Frank Downes

20th Century
Drama

Reading and Analysis

Acknowledgements

The author and publishers wish to thank the following for permission to use copyright material:

Faber & Faber for material from Sean O'Casey's *The Plough and the Stars* in *Sean O'Casey: Plays Two* (1986) pp. 127-39; Methuen for material from Debbie Horsfield's *True Dare Kiss* in *The Red Devils Trilogy* (1986) pp. 40-48 and 89-95, for material from Charlotte Keatley's *My Mother Said I Never Should* (1994) pp. 18-29, for material from Willy Russell's *Blood Brothers* in *Educating Rita with Blood Brothers and Stags and Hens* (1986) pp. 81-101, for material from Wole Soyinka's *Jero's Metamorphosis* in *Soyinka: Six Plays* (1984) pp. 67-86; Penguin Books for material from Arthur Miller's *A View from the Bridge* in *A View from the Bridge and All My Sons* (1990) pp. 42-58; Peters Fraser & Dunlop Group on behalf of Mike Leigh for material from Mike Leigh's *Abigail's Party* in *Abigail's Party and Goose Pimples* (Penguin Plays, 1983) pp. 19-26; The Random House Archive & Library for material from Alan Ayckbourn's *Absurd Person Singular* in *Alan Ayckbourn: Three Plays* (Penguin Drama, 1979) pp. 47-61; Tessa Sayle Agency for material from *A Taste of Honey* (Eyre Methuen, 1974) pp. 59-69.

The publisher would also like to acknowledge and thank the following sources for permission to reproduce production photographs:

Bill Kenwright Ltd/Alistair Muir, pages 9, 23; Catherine Ashmore, pages 52, 57, 60; Dominic Photography, pages 34, 73, 77; Donald Cooper/Photostage, pages 41, 80, 96, 105, 110, 134, 138; Heinemann and Ginn International/George Hallett, page 129.

Pearson Education Limited
Edinburgh Gate
Harlow
Essex
CM20 2JE

England and Associated Companies throughout the World

ISBN 0-582-34134-5

First published 2000

Printed in China

The Publisher's policy is to use paper manufactured from sustainable forests.

Contents

Introduction

The nature of drama

What are the essential elements of drama? Despite the enormous variety and range of plays, a number of features are always present:

- some form of a story
- some representation of character
- spectacle and action
- an audience and a theatrical space.

The purpose of this book is to look at the way in which post-1914 drama manages to keep to these basic features of drama. It focuses closely on the ways in which individual plays would be performed in the theatre, and also shows how such performance can contribute to an audience's understanding.

Post-1914 drama

Post-1914 drama is very interesting and contains many different types of plays. Many are quite challenging in terms of their ideas and attitudes. For example, one of our selected plays is the *The Plough and The Stars* by Sean O'Casey. When it was first produced in Dublin, this play caused riots because audiences felt that it presented a very bad picture of Irish people and more especially, those involved in political activity.

A realistic picture of the world is presented to audiences in post-1914 drama, and people can recognise aspects of their own lives. In recent years, many people who had never previously been to the theatre have begun to enjoy dramas by writers as varied as Arthur Miller and Willy Russell.

For many centuries men have written most of the plays performed in the theatre, but in the latter part of the twentieth century, many women have begun to write. This trend will certainly continue and in our selection we look at plays by important British female playwrights.

Another feature of post-1914 drama is the growing importance of writers from other cultures and in our collection we look at a play by the Nigerian writer, Wole Soyinka, who was the first black African to win the Nobel Prize for Literature.

Many of these plays introduce new ways of creating and performing. A good example in our selection is *Abigail's Party*. This was developed from an original idea by Mike Leigh, but developed through rehearsals and workshops by the cast of the first production. Out of this came a comic classic. Mike Leigh's approach to script-writing and directing has since been used with great success in film-making.

The best post-1914 drama:

- is realistic and relevant to our lives
- uses interesting language
- provides living and believable characters
- makes effective use of theatrical space
- challenges and entertains an audience.

The purpose of this book is to give you a chance to experience some of the qualities of post-1914 drama and to be able to write about them as part of your GCSE course.

The selection of plays

The plays in this book have been selected because they are interesting and enjoyable examples of post-1914 drama. The choice of plays has been made with the following ideas in mind:

Classic plays: Plays that have stood the test of time are considered to be 'classic' plays.

Accessible plays: Not all drama is difficult to appreciate. It is often very enjoyable and easy to grasp. Many modern popular plays are hugely entertaining.

Challenging plays: Some drama is controversial and challenging in terms of ideas and techniques. In many plays, the language, action and ideas have provoked strong reactions.

Plays written outside the UK: Our selection includes plays from Ireland, USA and Nigeria. Many great plays written in the English language are not written in Britain, and many new plays in Britain are now being written by writers from minority ethnic groups.

Plays written by women: It is often suggested that plays written by women have a different perspective on life, emphasising elements that are sometimes neglected in the works of male writers.

Tragedy and comedy: Western drama has been dominated over the centuries by tragedies (like Shakespeare's *Macbeth*) and comedies (like Shakespeare's *Twelfth Night*). We look at examples of both in our selection but post-1914 drama is not always easy to place in such categories. We therefore also look at plays that contain both tragic and comic elements.

Using this book for your GCSE

Post-1914 drama can be studied as part of a GCSE English Literature course, or for wider reading on some GCSE English syllabuses. Some plays may also be studied as part of the 'other cultures and traditions' element when this is offered as coursework (as in the present NEAB GCSE English, post-16).

You will need to show that you can respond to action, characters, dramatic devices and social and historical setting.

To get into the E Band at GCSE, you should be able to:

- recognise how character is revealed in dialogue and action
- describe effects of some dramatic devices or structures
- comment on social/historical setting of text.

To get into the C band, you should be able to:

- explore dramatic effects of character and action
- use detail to explore effects of dramatic devices and structures
- explore relevance of aspects of the social/historical setting of text.

And to get into the A band, you should be able to:

- evaluate dramatic effects of character and action
- analyse detail to evaluate effects of dramatic devices and structures
- sensitively evaluate relevant social/historical influences to analyse their importance to themes and meanings.

The structure of each chapter

Each chapter follows the same pattern and comprises:

Background and context: This puts the play into its historical and social context and gives some idea of the achievements of the writer.

Understanding action and structure: This section takes you into the story of the play (the plot) as well as helping you to see how this is put together (the structure).

Understanding character: This allows you to consider the words, actions and thoughts of the major characters from the excerpt.

Understanding themes: Many plays have important or challenging things to say. Here we explore the themes of the plays.

Understanding dramatic devices: This covers a huge range of features and includes such aspects as language, humour and contrast.

Understanding performance: Here we look closely at the features of the play that make it interesting to watch in the theatre. This includes costume and lighting, pace and movement, sets and design, and of course, acting itself.

Tasks: These are writing and practical activities, which will give you the chance to involve yourself with some acting of your own, as well as a range of other tasks.

Useful notes: In this section there are explanations of difficult words or phrases and specific comments on interesting or unusual features of language.

A variety of questions and tasks have been included in each chapter to help you to understand and appreciate each extract.

Popular Drama: *Blood Brothers* by Willy Russell

Background and context

Willy Russell was born in 1947 in Whiston, near Liverpool and his family moved to Liverpool when he was a boy. He had little idea of what he wanted to do and left school at 16 to work in a hairdresser's shop. However, he was not satisfied with this career and became a teacher. It was while training to become a teacher that he became interested in writing drama.

Russell's plays deal with working-class life and the ways in which people are shaped and sometimes limited by their environment. He is especially concerned with the importance of education and ambition in people's lives. Many of his plays are very humorous and he has a very good ear for working-class speech, something that he shares with many of the writers in this book (such as Sean O'Casey).

Blood Brothers is a musical. It is mainly entertainment but Russell's concerns are never far from the surface in his story of two twins, separated at birth only to find themselves drawn together in tragic circumstances. Like all of Russell's plays it shows tenderness, warmth and humour. The female characters are very strong as in many of Russell's plays. Written in the early 1980s when life on Merseyside was grim, Russell also comments on social divisions and poverty, as can be seen in this extract.

Blood Brothers

PRODUCTION NOTE

The setting for *Blood Brothers* is an open stage, with the different settings and time spans being indicated by lighting changes, with the minimum of properties and furniture. The whole play should flow along easily and smoothly, with no cumbersome scene changes. Two areas are semi-permanent — the Lyons house and the Johnstone house. We see the interior of the Lyons' comfortable home but usually only the exterior front door of the Johnstone house, with the 'interior' scenes taking place outside the door. The area between the two houses acts as communal ground for street scenes, park scenes, etc.

ACT ONE

The Overture comes to a close.

MRS JOHNSTONE *(singing):* Tell me it's not true

Say it's just a story.

The NARRATOR *steps forward.*

NARRATOR *(speaking):* So did y' hear the story of the Johnstone twins?

As like each other as two new pins,

Of one womb born, on the self same day,

How one was kept and one given away?

An' did you never hear how the Johnstones died,

Never knowing that they shared one name,

Till the day they died, when a mother cried

My own dear sons lie slain.

The Lights come up to show a re-enactment of the final moments of the play — the deaths of MICKEY *and* EDWARD. *The scene fades.*

MRS JOHNSTONE *enters with her back to the audience.*

An' did y' never hear of the mother, so cruel,

There's a stone in place of her heart?

Then bring her on and come judge for yourselves

How she came to play this part.

The NARRATOR *exits.*

Music is heard as MRS JOHNSTONE *turns and walks towards us. She is aged thirty but looks more like fifty.*

MRS JOHNSTONE *(singing):* Once I had a husband,

You know the sort of chap,

I met him at a dance and how he came on with the chat.

He said my eyes were deep blue pools,

My skin as soft as snow,

He told me I was sexier than Marilyn Monroe.

And we went dancing,

We went dancing.

Then, of course, I found

That I was six weeks overdue.

We got married at the registry an' then we had a 'do'.

We all had curly salmon sandwiches,

An' how the ale did flow,

They said the bride was lovelier than Marilyn Monroe.

And we went dancing,

Yes, we went dancing.

Bernie Nolan as Mrs Johnstone, on a 1998 tour of provincial theatres.

Then the baby came along,
We called him Darren Wayne,
Then three months on I found that I was in the club again.
An' though I still fancied dancing,
My husband wouldn't go,
With a wife he said was twice the size of Marilyn Monroe.

No more dancing
No more dancing.

By the time I was twenty-five,
I looked like forty-two,
With seven hungry mouths to feed and one more nearly due.
Me husband, he'd walked out on me,
A month or two ago,
For a girl they say who looks a bit like Marilyn Monroe.

And they go dancing
They go dancing

Yes they go dancing
They go…

An irate MILKMAN (*the* NARRATOR) *rushes in to rudely interrupt the song.*

MILKMAN: Listen love, I'm up to here with hard luck stories; you own me three pounds, seventeen and fourpence an' either you pay up today, like now, or I'll be forced to cut off your deliveries.

MRS JOHNSTONE: I said, I said, look, next week I'll pay y'…

MILKMAN: Next week, next week! Next week never arrives around here. I'd be a rich man if next week ever came.

MRS JOHNSTONE: But look, look, I start a job next week. I'll have money comin' in an' I'll be able to pay y'. Y' can't stop the milk. I need the milk. I'm pregnant.

MILKMAN: Well, don't look at me, love. I might be a milkman but it's got nothin' to do with me. Now you've been told, no money, no milk.

The MILKMAN *exits.*

MRS JOHNSTONE *stands alone and we hear some of her kids, off.*

KID ONE (*off*): Mam, Mam the baby's cryin'. He wants his bottle. Where's the milk?

KID TWO (*off*): 'Ey Mam, how come I'm on free dinners? All the other kids laugh at me.

KID THREE (off): 'Ey Mother, I'm starvin' an' there's nothin' in. There never bloody well is.

MRS JOHNSTONE (*perfunctorily*): Don't swear, I've told y'.

KID FOUR (*off*): Mum, I can't sleep, I'm hungry, I'm starvin'…

KIDS (*off*): An' me, Mam. An' me. An' me.

MRS JOHNSTONE (singing): I know it's hard on all you kids,
But try and get some sleep.
Next week I'll be earnin',
We'll have loads of things to eat,

We'll have ham, an' jam, an' spam an'

(*Speaking.*) Roast Beef, Yorkshire Puddin', Battenberg Cake, Chicken an' Chips, Corned Beef, Sausages, Treacle Tart, Mince an' Spuds, Milk Shake for the Baby:

There is a chorus of groaning ecstasy from the KIDS.

MRS JOHNSTONE *picks up the tune again.*

When I bring home the dough,

We'll live like kings, like bright young things,

Like Marilyn Monroe.

And we'll go dancing…

MRS JOHNSTONE *hums a few bars of the song, and dances a few steps, as she makes her way to her place of work —*

MRS LYONS' *house. During the dance she acquires a brush, dusters and a mop bucket.*

MRS LYONS' house *where* MRS JOHNSTONE *is working.* MRS LYONS *enters, carrying a parcel.*

MRS LYONS: Hello, Mrs Johnstone, how are you? Is the job working out all right for you?

MRS JOHNSTONE: It's, erm, great. Thank you. It's such a lovely house it's a pleasure to clean it.

MRS LYONS: It's a pretty house isn't it? It's a pity it's so big. I'm finding it rather large at present.

MRS JOHNSTONE: Oh. Yeh. With Mr Lyons being away an' that? When does he come back, Mrs Lyons?

MRS LYONS: Oh, it seems such a long time. The Company sent him out there for nine months, so, what's that, he'll be back in about five months' time.

MRS JOHNSTONE: Ah, you'll be glad when he's back won't you? The house won't feel so empty then, will it?

MRS LYONS *begins to unwrap her parcel.*

MRS LYONS: Actually, Mrs J, we bought such a large house for the — for the children — we thought children would come along.

MRS JOHNSTONE: Well y' might still be able to.

MRS LYONS: No, I'm afraid… We've been trying for such a long time now… I wanted to adopt but… Mr Lyons is… well he says he wanted his own son, not someone else's. Myself, I believe that an adopted child can become one's own.

MRS JOHNSTONE: Ah yeh… yeh. Ey, It's weird though, isn't it. Here's you can't have kids, an' me, I can't stop havin' them. Me husband used to say that all we had to do was shake hands and I'd be in the club. He must have shook hands with me before he left. I'm havin' another one y' know.

MRS LYONS: Oh, I see...

MRS JOHNSTONE: Oh but look, look it's all right, Mrs Lyons, I'll still be able to do me work. Havin' babies, it's like clockwork to me. I'm back on me feet an' workin' the next day y' know. If I have this one at the weekend I won't even need to take one day off. I love this job, y' know. We can just manage to get by now —

She is stopped by MRS LYONS *putting the contents of the package, a pair of new shoes, on to the table.*

Jesus Christ, Mrs Lyons, what are y' trying to do?

MRS LYONS: My God, what's wrong?

MRS JOHNSTONE: The shoes… the shoes…

MRS LYONS: Pardon?

MRS JOHNSTONE: New shoes on the table, take them off…

MRS LYONS *does so.*

(Relieved) Oh God, Mrs Lyons, never put new shoes on a table… You never know what'll happen.

MRS LYONS *(twigging it; laughing):* Oh… you mean you're superstitious?

MRS .JOHNSTONE: No, but you never put new shoes on the table.

MRS LYONS: Oh go on with you. Look, if it will make you any happier I'll put them away…

MRS LYONS *exits with the shoes.*

Music is heard as MRS JOHNSTONE *warily approaches the table and the NARRATOR enters.*

NARRATOR: There's shoes upon the table an' a joker in the pack, The salt's been spilled and a looking glass cracked, There's one lone magpie overhead.

MRS JOHNSTONE: I'm not superstitious.

NARRATOR: The Mother said.

MRS JOHNSTONE: I'm not superstitious.

NARRATOR: The Mother said.

The NARRATOR *exits to re-enter as a GYNAECOLOGIST.*

MRS JOHNSTONE: What are you doin' here? The milk bill's not due till Thursday.

GYNAECOLOGIST *(producing a listening funnel):* Actually I've given up the milk round and gone into medicine. I'm your gynaecologist. *(He begins to examine her.)* OK, Mummy, let's have a little listen to the baby's ticker, shall we?

MRS JOHNSTONE: I was dead worried about havin' another baby, you know, Doctor. I didn't see how we were gonna manage with another mouth to feed. But now I've got me a little job we'll be OK. If I'm careful we can just scrape by, even with another mouth to feed.

The GYNAECOLOGIST completes his examination.

GYNAECOLOGIST: Mouths, Mummy.

MRS JOHNSTONE: What?

GYNAECOLOGIST: Plural, Mrs Johnstone. Mouths to feed. You're expecting twins. Congratulations. And the next one please, Nurse.

The GYNAECOLOGIST exits.

MRS JOHNSTONE, *numbed by the news, moves back to her work, dusting the table upon which the shoes had been placed.*

MRS LYONS enters.

MRS LYONS: Hello, Mrs. J. How are you?

There is no reply.

(Registering the silence) Mrs J? Anything wrong?

MRS JOHNSTONE: I had it all worked out.

MRS LYONS: What's the matter?

MRS JOHNSTONE: We were just getting straight.

MRS LYONS: Why don't you sit down.

MRS JOHNSTONE: With one more baby we could have managed. But not with two. The Welfare have already been on to me. They say I'm incapable of controllin' the kids I've already got. They say I should put some of them into care. But I won't. I love the bones of every one of them. I'll even love these two when they come along. But like they say at the Welfare, kids can't live on love alone.

MRS LYONS: Twins? You're expecting twins?

The NARRATOR enters.

NARRATOR: How quickly an idea, planted, can

Take root and grow into a plan.

The thought conceived in this very room

Grew as surely as a seed, in a mother's womb.

The NARRATOR exits.

MRS LYONS *(almost inaudibly):* Give one to me.

MRS JOHNSTONE: What?

MRS LYONS *(containing her excitement):* Give one of them to me.

MRS JOHNSTONE: Give one to you?

MRS LYONS: Yes... yes.

MRS JOHNSTONE *(taking it almost as a joke):* But y' can't just...

MRS LYONS: When are you due?

MRS JOHNSTONE: Erm, well about... Oh, but Mrs...

MRS LYONS: Quickly, quickly tell me... when are you due?

MRS JOHNSTONE: July he said, the beginning of...

MRS LYONS: July... and my husband doesn't get back until, the middle of July. He need never guess...

MRS JOHNSTONE *(amused):* Oh, it's mad...

MRS LYONS: I know, it is. It's mad... but it's wonderful, it's perfect. Look, look, you're what, four months pregnant, but you're only just beginning to show... so, so I'm four months pregnant and I'm only just beginning to show. *(She grabs a cushion and arranges it beneath her dress.)* Look, look. I could have got pregnant just before he went away. But I didn't tell him in case I miscarried, I didn't want to worry him whilst he was away. But when he arrives home I tell him we were wrong, the doctors were wrong. I have a baby, our baby. Mrs Johnstone, it will work, it will if only you'll...

MRS JOHNSTONE: Oh, Mrs Lyons, you can't be serious.

MRS LYONS: You said yourself, you said you had too many children already.

MRS JOHNSTONE: Yeh, but I don't know if I wanna give one away.

MRS LYONS: Already you're being threatened by the Welfare people. Mrs Johnstone, with two more children how can you possibly avoid some of them being put into care? Surely, it's better to give one child to me. Look, at least if the child was with me you'd be able to see him every day, as you came to work.

MRS LYONS *stares at* MRS JOHNSTONE, *willing her to agree.*

Please, Mrs Johnstone. Please.

MRS JOHNSTONE: Are y'... are y' that desperate to have a baby?

MRS LYONS *(singing):* Each day I look out from this window,

I see him with his friends, I hear him call,

I rush down but as I fold my arms around him,

He's gone. Was he ever there at all?

I've dreamed of all the places I would take him,

The games we'd play the stories I would tell,

The jokes we'd share, the clothing I would make him,

I reach out. But as I do. He fades away.

The melody shifts into that of MRS JOHNSTONE *who is looking at* MRS LYONS, *feeling for her.* MRS LYONS *gives a half smile and a shrug, perhaps slightly embarrassed at what she has revealed.* MRS JOHNSTONE *turns and looks at the room she is in. Looking up in awe at the comparative opulence and ease of the place. Tentatively and wondering she sings.*

MRS JOHNSTONE: If my child was raised

In a palace like this one,

(He) wouldn't have to worry where

His next meal was comin' from.

His clothing would be (supplied by)

George Henry Lee.

MRS LYONS *sees that* MRS JOHNSTONE *might be persuaded.*

MRS LYONS *(singing):* He'd have all his own toys

And a garden to play in.

MRS JOHNSTONE: He could make too much noise

Without the neighbours complainin'.

MRS LYONS: Silver trays to take meals on

MRS JOHNSTONE: A bike with *both* wheels on?

MRS LYONS *nods enthusiastically.*

MRS LYONS: And he'd sleep every night

In a bed of his own.

MRS JOHNSTONE: He wouldn't get into fights

He'd leave matches alone.

And you'd never find him

Effin' and blindin'.

And when he grew up

He could never be told

To stand and queue up

For hours on end at the dole

He'd grow up to be

MRS LYONS

MRS JOHNSTONE $\Big\}$ *(together)* A credit to me

MRS JOHNSTONE: To you.

MRS JOHNSTONE: I would still be able to see him every day, wouldn't I?

MRS LYONS: Of course.

MRS JOHNSTONE: An'… an' you would look after him, wouldn't y'?

MRS LYONS *(singing):* I'd keep him warm in the winter

And cool when it shines.

I'd pull out his splinters

Without making him cry.

I'd always be there

If his dream was a nightmare.

My child.

My child.

There is a pause before MRS JOHNSTONE *nods.* MRS LYONS *goes across and kisses her, hugs her.* MRS JOHNSTONE *is slightly embarrassed.*

Oh. Now you must help me. There's so much… I'll have to… *(She takes out the cushion.)* We'll do this properly so that it's thoroughly convincing, and I'll need to see you walk, and baby clothes, I'll have to knit and buy bottles and suffer from piles.

MRS JOHNSTONE: What?

MRS LYONS: Doesn't one get piles when one's pregnant? And buy a cot and… Oh help me with this, Mrs J. Is it in the right place? *(She puts the cushion back again.)* I want it to look right before I go shopping.

MRS JOHNSTONE *(helping her with the false pregnancy):* What you goin' the shops for? I do the shopping.

MRS LYONS: Oh no, from now on I do the shopping. I want everyone to know about my baby. *(She suddenly reaches for the Bible.)*

Music.

Mrs J. We must make this a, erm, a binding agreement.

MRS LYONS *shows the Bible to* MRS JOHNSTONE, *who is at first reluctant and then lays her hand on it.*

The NARRATOR *enters. A bass note, repeated as a heartbeat.*

NARRATOR: In the name of Jesus, the thing was done,

Now there's no going back, for anyone.

It's too late now, for feeling torn

There's a pact been sealed, there's a deal been born.

MRS LYONS *puts the Bible away.* MRS JOHNSTONE *stands and stares as* MRS LYONS *grabs shopping bags and takes a last satisfied glance at herself in the mirror.*

MRS JOHNSTONE: Why… why did we have to do that?

MRS LYONS: Mrs J, nobody must ever know. Therefore we have to have an agreement.

MRS JOHNSTONE *nods but is still uncomfortable.*

Right, I shan't be long. Bye.

MRS LYONS *exits.*

MRS JOHNSTONE *stands alone, afraid.*

The heartbeat grows in intensity.

NARRATOR: How swiftly those who've made a pact,

Can come to overlook the fact.

Or wish the reckoning to be delayed

But a debt is a debt, and must be paid.

The NARRATOR *exits.*

As the heartbeat reaches maximum volume it suddenly stops and is replaced by the sound of crying babies.

Two nurses appear, each carrying a bundle. A pram is wheeled on.

The nurses hand the bundles to MRS JOHNSTONE *who places them smiling, into the pram. Making faces and noises at the babies she stops the crying. The babies settled, she sets off, wheeling the pram towards home.*

Various debt collectors emerge from her house to confront MRS JOHNSTONE.

CATALOGUE MAN: I'm sorry love… the kids said you were at the hospital. *(He looks into the pram.)* Ah… they're lovely, aren't they? I'm sorry love, especially at a time like this, but, you are twelve weeks behind in your payments. I've got to do this, girl…

FINANCE MAN: Y' shouldn't sign for the bloody stuff, missis. If y' know y' can't pay, y' shouldn't bloody well sign.

CATALOGUE MAN: Look, if y' could give me a couple of weeks' money on this I could leave it.

MRS JOHNSTONE *shakes her head.*

FINANCE MAN: Y' shouldn't have signed for all this stuff, should y'? Y' knew y' wouldn't be able to pay, didn't y'?

MRS JOHNSTONE *(almost to herself):* When I got me job, I thought I would be able to pay. When I went in the showroom I only meant to come out with a couple of things. But when you're standing there, it all looks so nice. When y' look in the catalogue an' there's six months to pay, it seems years away, an' y' need a few things so y' sign.

FINANCE MAN: Yeh, well y' bloody well shouldn't.

MRS JOHNSTONE *(coming out of her trance; angrily):* I know I shouldn't, you soft get. I've spent all me bleedin' life knowin' I *shouldn't.* But I do. Now, take y' soddin' wireless and get off.

CATALOGUE MAN: Honest love, I'm sorry.

MRS JOHNSTONE: It's all right lad… we're used to it. We were in the middle of our tea one night when they arrived for the table. *(She gives a wry laugh.)*

CATALOGUE MAN: Ah well as long as y' can laugh about it, eh, that's the main thing isn't it?

The CATALOGUE MAN *exits.*

MRS JOHNSTONE *(not laughing):* Yeh.

Other creditors continue to enter the house and leave with goods.

MRS JOHNSTONE *watches the creditors. The babies begin to cry and she moves to the pram, rocking it gently as she sings, as if to the babies in the pram. (Singing)*

Only mine until
The time comes round
To pay the bill.
Then, I'm afraid,
What can't be paid
Must be returned.
You never, ever learn,
That nothing's yours,
On easy terms.

Only for a time,
I must not learn,
To call you mine.
Familiarize
That face, those eyes
Make future plans
That cannot be confirmed.
On borrowed time,
On easy terms.

Living on the never never,
Constant as the changing weather,
Never sure

Who's at the door
Or the price I'll have to pay.
Should we meet again
I will not recognize your name.
You can be sure
What's gone before
Will be concealed.
Your friends will never learn
That once we were
On easy terms.

Living on the never never,
Constant as the changing weather,
Never sure
Who's at the door
Or the price I'll have to pay...
MRS LYONS *enters, still with the pregnancy padding.*
MRS LYONS: They're born, you didn't notify me.
MRS JOHNSTONE: Well I... I just... it's... couldn't I keep them for a few more days, please, please, they're a pair, they go together.
MRS LYONS: My husband is due back tomorrow, Mrs Johnstone. I must have my baby. We made an agreement, a bargain. You swore on the Bible.
MRS JOHNSTONE: You'd better... you'd better see which one you want.
MRS LYONS: I'll take...
MRS JOHNSTONE: No. Don't tell me which one. Just take him, take him. *(Singing)*
Living on the never never,
Constant as the changing weather,
Never sure
Who's at the door
Or the price I'll have to pay,
Should we meet again...

MRS LYONS *rapidly pulls out the padding from beneath her dress. Amongst it is a shawl which she uses to wrap around the baby before picking it up from the pram.*

MRS LYONS: Thank you Mrs Johnstone, thank you. I'll see you next week.
MRS JOHNSTONE: I'm due back tomorrow.
MRS LYONS: I know but why don't you... why don't you take the week off, on full pay of course.
MRS LYON *exits.*
MRS JOHNSTONE *turns and enters her house with the remaining twin in the pram.*
KID ONE *(off):* What happened to the other twin, Mother?
KID TWO *(off):* Where's the other twinny, Mam?
MRS JOHNSTONE: He's gone. He's gone up to heaven, love. He's living with Jesus and the angels.
KID THREE *(off):* What's it like there Mam, in heaven?

MRS JOHNSTONE: It's lovely son, he'll be well looked after there. He'll have anything he wants.

KID ONE (off): Will he have his own bike?

MRS JOHNSTONE: Yeh. With both wheels on.

KID ONE (off): Why can't I have a bike? Eh?

MRS JOHNSTONE: I'll… I'll have a look in the catalogue next week. We'll see what the bikes are like in there.

KIDS (together, off): Mam, I want a Meccano set.

You said I could have a new dress, Mother.

Why can't I have an air pistol?

Let's look in the catalogue now, Mam.

It's great when we look in the catalogue, Mam.

Go on, let's all look in the catalogue.

MRS JOHNSTONE: I've told y', when I get home, I've got to go to work.

MR *and* MRS LYONS *enter their house and we see them looking at the child in its cot.*

MRS JOHNSTONE *enters and immediately goes about her work.*

MRS JOHNSTONE *stops work for a moment and glances into the cot, beaming and cooing.* MR LYONS *is next to her with* MRS LYONS *in the background, obviously agitated at* MRS JOHNSTONE's *fussing.*

Aw, he's really comin' on now, isn't he, Mr Lyons? I'll bet y' dead proud of him, aren't y', aren't y', eh?

MR LYONS (good naturedly): Yes… yes I am, aren't I Edward? I'm proud of Jennifer, too.

MR LYONS *beams at his wife who can hardly raise a smile.*

MRS JOHNSTONE: Ah… he's lovely. (She coos into the cot.) Ah look, he wants to be picked up, I'll just…

MRS LYONS: No, no, Mrs Johnstone. He's fine. He doesn't want to be picked up.

MRS JOHNSTONE: Ah, but look he's gonna cry…

MRS LYONS: If he needs picking up I shall pick him up. All right?

MRS JOHNSTONE: Well, I just thought, I'm sorry I…

MRS LYONS: Yes. Erm, has the bathroom been done? Time is getting on.

MRS JOHNSTONE: Oh. Yeh, yeh…

MRS JOHNSTONE *exits.*

MR LYONS: Darling. Don't be hard on the woman. She only wanted to hold the baby. All women like to hold babies, don't they?

MRS LYONS: I don't want her to hold the baby, Richard. She's… I don't want the baby to catch anything. Babies catch things very easily, Richard.

MR LYONS: All right, all right, you know best.

MRS LYONS: You don't see her as much as I do. She's always fussing over him; any opportunity and she's cooing and cuddling as if she were his mother. She's always bothering him, Richard, always. Since the baby arrived she ignores most of her work. (She is about to cry.)

MR LYONS: Come on, come on… It's all right Jennifer. You're just a little… it's this depression thing that happens after a woman's had a…

MRS LYONS: I'm not depressed Richard; it's just that she makes me feel… Richard, I think she should go.

MR LYONS: And what will you do for help in the house?

MRS LYONS: I'll find somebody else. I'll find somebody who doesn't spend all day fussing over the baby.

MR LYONS (*glancing at his watch*): Oh well, I suppose you know best. The house is your domain. Look, Jen, I've got a board meeting. I really must dash.

MRS LYONS: Richard, can you let me have some cash?

MR LYONS: Of course.

MRS LYONS: I need about fifty pounds.

MR LYONS: My God, what for?

MRS LYONS: I've got lots of things to buy for the baby, I've got the nursery to sort out…

MR LYONS: All right, all right, here. (*He hands her the money.*) MR LYONS *exits.*

MRS LYONS *considers what she is about to do and then calls*

MRS LYONS: Mrs Johnstone. Mrs Johnstone, would you come out here for a moment, please.

MRS JOHNSTONE *enters.*

MRS JOHNSTONE: Yes?

MRS LYONS. Sit down. Richard and I have been talking it over and, well the thing is, we both think it would be better if you left.

MRS JOHNSTONE: Left where?

MRS LYONS: It's your work. Your work has deteriorated.

MRS JOHNSTONE: But, I work the way I've always worked.

MRS LYONS: Well, I'm sorry, we're not satisfied.

MRS JOHNSTONE: What will I do? How are we gonna live without my job?

MRS LYONS: Yes, well we've thought of that. Here, here's… (*She pushes the money into* MRS JOHNSTONE'*s hand.*) it's a lot of money… but, well…

MRS JOHNSTONE (*thinking, desperate. Trying to get it together.*) OK. All right. All right, Mrs Lyons, right. If I'm goin', I'm takin' my son with me, I'm takin'…

As MRS JOHNSTONE *moves towards the cot* MRS LYONS *roughly drags her out of the way.*

MRS LYONS: Oh no, you're not. Edward is my son. Mine.

MRS JOHNSTONE: I'll tell someone… I'll tell the police

I'll bring the police in an'…

MRS LYONS: No… no you won't. You gave your baby away.

Don't you realize what a crime that is. You'll be locked up. You sold your baby.

MRS JOHNSTONE, *horrified, sees the bundle of notes in her hand, and throws it across the room.*

MRS JOHNSTONE: I didn't… you told me, you said I could see him every day. Well, I'll tell someone, I'm gonna tell…

MRS JOHNSTONE *starts to leave but* MRS LYONS *stops her.*

MRS LYONS: No. You'll tell nobody.

Music.

Because… because If you tell anyone… and these children learn of the truth, then you know what will happen, don't you? You do know what they say about twins, secretly parted, don't you?

MRS JOHNSTONE (*terrified*): What? What?

MRS LYONS: They say… they say that if either twin learns that he once was a pair, they shall both immediately die. It means, Mrs Johnstone, that these brothers shall grow up, unaware of the other's existence. They shall be raised apart and never, ever told what was once the truth. You won't tell anyone about this, Mrs Johnstone, because if you do, you will kill them.

MRS LYONS *picks up the money and thrusts it into* MRS JOHNSTONE's *hands.*
MRS LYONS *turns and walks away.*
The NARRATOR *enters*
NARRATOR *(singing):* Shoes upon the table
An' a spider's been killed.
Someone broke the lookin' glass
A full moon shinin'
An' the salt's been spilled.
You're walkin' on the pavement cracks
Don't know what's gonna come to pass.

Now y' know the devil's got your number,
Y' know he's gonna find y',
Y' know he's right behind y',
He's starin' through your windows
He's creepin' down the hall.

Ain't no point in clutching
At your rosary
You're always gonna know what was done
Even when you shut your eyes you still see
That you sold a son
And you can't tell anyone.

But y' know the devil's got your number,
Y' know he's gonna find y',
Y' know he's right behind y',
He's starin' through your windows
He's creeping down the hall

Yes, y' know the devil's got your number
He's gonna find y',
Y' know he's right behind y',
He's standin' on your step
And he's knocking at your door.
He's knocking at your door,
He's knocking at your door.
The NARRATOR *exits.*

During the song MRS JOHNSTONE *has gone to her house and locked herself in.*
MICKEY, *aged 'seven' is knocking incessantly at the door. He is carrying a toy gun.*
MRS JOHNSTONE *(screaming; off):* Go away!
MICKEY: Mother… will y' open the bleedin' door or what?

MRS JOHNSTONE *(realizing; with relief; off)*: Mickey?

MRS JOHNSTONE *comes to open the door.*

MICKEY: Mam, Mam.

She grabs him and hugs him. He extricates himself.

Why was the door bolted? Did you think it was the rent man?

She laughs and looks at him.

Mam, our Sammy's robbed me other gun an' that was me best one. Why does he rob all me things off me?

MRS JOHNSTONE: Because you're the youngest Mickey. It used to happen to our Sammy when he was the youngest.

MICKEY: Mam, we're playin' mounted police an' Indians. I'm a mountie. Mam, Mam, y' know this mornin', we've wiped out three thousand Indians.

MRS JOHNSTONE: Good.

MICKEY *(aiming the gun at her and firing)*: Mam, Mam, you're dead.

MRS JOHNSTONE *(staring at him)*: Hmm.

MICKEY: What's up, Mam?

MRS JOHNSTONE: Nothin' son. Go on, you go out an' play, there's a good lad. But, ey, don't you go playin' with those hooligans down at the rough end.

MICKEY *(on his way out)*: We're down at the other end, near the big houses in the park.

MRS JOHNSTONE: Mickey! Come here.

MICKEY: What?

MRS JOHNSTONE: What did you say, where have you been playin'?

MICKEY: Mam, I'm sorry, I forgot.

MRS JOHNSTONE: What have I told you about playin' up near there. Come here. *(She grabs him.)*

MICKEY: It wasn't my fault. Honest.

MRS JOHNSTONE: So whose fault was it then?

MICKEY: The Indians. They rode up that way, they were tryin' to escape.

MRS JOHNSTONE: Don't you ever go up there. Do you hear me?

MICKEY: Yeh. You let our Sammy go up there.

MRS JOHNSTONE: Our Sammy's older than you.

MICKEY: But why…

MRS .JOHNSTONE: Just shut up. Never mind why. You don't go up near there. Now go on, get out an' play. But you stay outside the front door where I can see y'.

MICKEY: Ah but, Mam, the…

MRS JOHNSTONE: Go on!

MRS JOHNSTONE *exits.*

MICKEY *makes his way outside. He is fed up. Desultory.*

Shoots down a few imaginary Indians but somehow the magic

has gone out of genocide.

MICKEY *sits, bored, looking at the ants on the pavement.*

MICKEY *(reciting)*: I wish I was our Sammy

Our Sammy's nearly ten.

He's got two worms and a catapult

An' he's built a underground den.

But I'm not allowed to go in there,

I have to stay near the gate,
'Cos me Mam says I'm only seven,
But I'm not, I'm nearly eight!

I sometimes hate our Sammy,
He robbed me toy car y' know,
Now the wheels are missin' an' the top's broke off,
An' the bleedin' thing won't go.
An' he said when he took it, it was just like that,
But it wasn't, it went dead straight,
But y' can't say nott'n when they think y' seven
An' y' not, y' nearly eight.

I wish I was our Sammy,
Y' wanna see him spit,
Straight in y' eye from twenty yards
An' every time a hit.
He's allowed to play with matches,
And he goes to bed dead late,
And I have to go at seven,
Even though I'm nearly eight.

Y' know our Sammy,
He draws nudey women,
Without arms, or legs, or even heads
in the baths, when he goes swimmin'.
But I'm not allowed to go to the baths,
Me Mam says I have to wait,
'Cos I might get drowned, 'cos I'm only seven,
But I'm not, I'm nearly eight.

Y' know our Sammy,
Y' know what he sometimes does?
He wees straight through the letter box
Of the house next door to us.
I tried to do it one night,
But I had to stand on a crate,
'Cos I couldn't reach the letter box
But I will by the time I'm eight.

Bored and petulant, MICKEY *sits and shoots an imaginary Sammy.*
EDWARD, *also aged 'seven' appears. He is bright and forthcoming.*
EDWARD: Hello.
MICKEY *(suspiciously):* Hello.
EDWARD: I've seen you before.
MICKEY: Where?

Mickey (Stephen Palfreman) and Edward (Mark Hutchinson) meet on the street in a production at the Phoenix Theatre, 1988.

EDWARD: You were playing with some other boys near my house.

MICKEY: Do you live up in the park?

EDWARD: Yes. Are you going to come and play up there again?

MICKEY: No. I would do but I'm not allowed.

EDWARD: Why?

MICKEY: 'Cos me mam says.

EDWARD: Well, my mummy doesn't allow me to play down here actually.

MICKEY: 'Gis a sweet.

EDWARD: All right. *(He offers a bag from his pocket.)*

MICKEY *(shocked):* What?

EDWARD: Here.

MICKEY *(trying to work out the catch. Suspiciously taking one)*

Can I have another one. For our Sammy?

EDWARD: Yes, of course. Take as many as you want.

MICKEY *(taking a handful):* Are you soft?

EDWARD: I don't think so.

MICKEY: Round here if y' ask for a sweet, y' have to ask about, about twenty million times. An' y' know what?

EDWARD *(sitting beside MICKEY):* What?

MICKEY: They still don't bleedin' give y' one. Sometimes our Sammy does but y' have to be dead careful if our Sammy gives y' a sweet.

EDWARD: Why?

MICKEY: 'Cos, if our Sammy gives y' a sweet he's usually weed on it first.

EDWARD *(exploding in giggles):* Oh, that sounds like super fun.

MICKEY: It is. If y' our Sammy.

EDWARD: Do you want to come and play?

MICKEY: I might do. But I'm not playin' now 'cos I'm pissed off.

EDWARD *(awed):* Pissed off. You say smashing things don't you? Do you know any more words like that?

MICKEY: Yeh. Yeh, I know loads of words like that. Y' know, like the 'F' word.

EDWARD *(clueless):* Pardon?

MICKEY: The 'F' word.

EDWARD is *still puzzled.* MICKEY *looks round to check that he cannot be overheard, then whispers the word to* EDWARD.

The two of them immediately wriggle and giggle with glee.

EDWARD: What does it mean?

MICKEY: I don't know. It sounds good though, doesn't it?

EDWARD: Fantastic. When I get home I'll look it up in the dictionary.

MICKEY: In the what?

EDWARD: The dictionary. Don't you know what a dictionary is?

MICKEY: 'Course I do… It's a, it's a thingy innit?

EDWARD: A book which explains the meaning of words.

MICKEY: The meaning of words, yeh. Our Sammy'll be here soon. I hope he's in a good mood. He's dead mean sometimes.

EDWARD: Why?

MICKEY: It's 'cos he's got a plate in his head.

EDWARD: A plate. In his head?

MICKEY: Yeh. When he was little, me Mam was at work an' our Donna Marie was supposed to be lookin' after him but he fell out the window an' broke his head. So they took him to the hospital an' put a plate in his head.

EDWARD: A plate. A dinner plate?

MICKEY: I don't think so, 'cos our Sammy's head's not really that big. I think it must have been one of them little plates that you have bread off.

EDWARD: A side plate?

MICKEY: No, it's on the top.

EDWARD: And… and can you see the shape of it, in his head?

MICKEY: I suppose, I suppose if y' looked under his hair.

EDWARD *(after a reflective pause):* You know the most smashing things. Will you be my best friend?

MICKEY: Yeh. If y' want.

EDWARD: What's your name?

MICKEY: Michael Johnstone. But everyone calls me Mickey. What's yours?

EDWARD: Edward Lyons.

MICKEY: D' they call y' Eddie?

EDWARD: No.

MICKEY: Well, I will.

EDWARD: Will you?

MICKEY: Yeh. How old are y' Eddie?

EDWARD: Seven.

MICKEY: I'm older than you. I'm nearly eight.

EDWARD: Well, I'm nearly eight, really.

MICKEY: What's your birthday?

EDWARD: July the eighteenth.

MICKEY: So is mine.

EDWARD: Is it really?

MICKEY: Ey, we were born on the same day… that means we can be blood brothers. Do you wanna be my blood brother, Eddie?

EDWARD: Yes, please.

MICKEY *(producing a penknife):* It hurts y' know. *(He puts a nick in his hand.)* Now, give us yours.

MICKEY *nicks* EDWARD*'s hand, then they clamp hands together.*

See this means that we're blood brothers, an' that we always have to stand by each other. Now you say after me: 'I will always defend my brother'.

EDWARD: I will always defend my brother…

MICKEY: And stand by him.

EDWARD: And stand by him.

MICKEY: An' share all my sweets with him.

EDWARD: And share…

SAMMY *leaps in front of them, gun in his hand, pointed at them.*

Understanding action and structure

The play concerns itself with the lives of twins, separated shortly after birth and raised in two families, one poor and one well-off. We see their progress from childhood into early adulthood. It is a fast moving and entertaining story which ends tragically, as is shown silently in the opening scene of the play.

The scene we are reading looks closely at the arrangements that lead to Mrs Johnstone giving away one of her children.

- Why does Mrs Johnstone feel under pressure in this scene?
- What are Mrs Lyons feelings towards Mrs Johnstone?
- Why does Mrs Lyons want Mrs Johnstone to give her one of her children?

As the scene progresses, Mr Lyons becomes involved and problems emerge for Mrs Johnstone.

- What is Mr Lyons' response to events?
- Find two examples where Mrs Lyons surprises Mrs Johnstone.
- How does Mrs Lyons threaten Mrs Johnstone?

Seven years later, Mrs Johnstone's family is growing up but their lives are still difficult. The two boys, Mickey and Edward, meet, not knowing their backgrounds. However their seemingly different lives don't stop them from becoming friends. They find time to play with each other and cement their relationship by going through a very simple ceremony that gives the play its title.

- What instruction has Mrs Johstone given to Mickey about his playing?
- Why has she given this instruction?
- Why do the boys become 'blood brothers'?

Understanding character

The main characters in this scene are:

the Narrator

Mrs Johnstone

Mrs Lyons

Mr Lyons

Mickey

Edward (Eddie)

Sam.

Mrs Johnstone is a woman on whom the woes of the world have fallen. At the start of the play she finds it difficult to feed her family and has been forced to find a job that will bring in some money. As she has such a hard time, she is forced to cut corners and difficulties with money continue to get her into scrapes.

- What do you think the following lines show us of Mrs Johnstone's character?

> I know it's hard on all you kids,
> But try and get some sleep.
> Next week I'll be earnin',
> We'll have loads of things to eat,
> We'll have ham, an' jam, an' spam an'…

Mrs Lyons is in a far better situation than Mrs Johnstone but feels very frustrated at her lack of children. Her behaviour reveals a hard, possibly ruthless streak.

- Look at the conversation between Mrs Lyons and her husband. What does this tell us about her?

Mickey is a typical working-class young boy whose main concerns are play and more play. He is also bothered about his elder brother, Sammy.

Look at the section beginning:

> I wish I was our Sammy
> Our Sammy's nearly ten.
> He's got two worms and a catapult
> An' he's built a underground den.

- What you think is the main feeling that comes across?

Edward, Mickey's twin brother, lives a different kind of life but wants to play and to meet other boys. In this scene, what is it about Mickey that intrigues Edward so much?

Understanding themes

This entertaining play covers several important themes.

Social class

- What differences are there between the lives of Mrs Johnstone and Mrs Lyons?

Look at:

a) money

b) attitudes

c) language

d) relationships.

Marriage

Mrs Johnstone's first song tells us about her marriage and children.

- What are the key events that are described in this song?
- How do her experiences compare with the main aspects of the Lyons' marriage?

Childhood

Childhood games and relationships take the spotlight in the latter parts of this scene. Mickey's song on page 21, beginning 'I wish I was our Sammy' is an entertaining picture of childhood. However, some aspects of childhood activity are reflected in adult life, to devastating effect.

- What features of Mickey's playing does Russell emphasise in the following section on page 20 from:

'MICKEY, *aged 'seven' is knocking incessantly at the door.*'

down to

'MICKEY: (*aiming the gun at her and firing*) Mam, Mam, you're dead.'

Luck or fortune

Russell's play relies on a number of coincidences and accidents that help the story to move along. However, there is a serious point here. What he is trying to say is that it is not in our power to determine who our parents are, or who we might meet in life and yet this has a tremendous impact on what happens to us.

- Look again at the scene. What features could be considered a matter of luck?

Blood brothers

The theme of a friendship that is special is very important in this play and has appeared in other Russell plays, in different forms. The linking of Mickey and Edward contrasts with the split between Mrs Johnstone and Mrs Lyons.

Understanding dramatic devices

Language

The language of the play is exactly suited to its purpose in a musical play. It is varied, entertaining and not difficult to understand. However some features of the language stand out.

Contrast

- Look at the conversations between Mrs Johnstone and Mrs Lyons, and between Mickey and Edward. Is there any difference in the way they talk?

Slang and dialect

- Russell has a very sensitive ear to the speech of working-class people and uses a variety of ways to bring this into his play. Find some examples of slang and dialect in this scene.

Language and children

- Russell wants to create a sense of childhood and youth in this play and he succeeds in doing this. Look again at the conversation between Mickey and Edward that concludes our scene and see if you can find examples of the way children talk to each other.

Humour

This is a very important aspect of Russell's writing. The humour provides a great deal of the character and warmth of the play. There are many examples on every page but it is useful to consider some of the different kinds of humour that he uses.

Wit

This kind of humour is where there is a play on ideas, as in the following:

> MRS JOHNSTONE: …I'm pregnant.
> MILKMAN: Well, don't look at me, love. I might be a milkman but it's got nothin' to do with me.

Jokes

- Look at the 'plate in his head' joke on page 24 and how it is developed. Find some other examples of good jokes in the scene.

Surprise and shock

- What surprising event is treated humorously in this scene?

Use of language

Language is the source of many of the humorous features of the play. Russell is particularly fond of making fun of people when they take airs and graces.

- For instance, why is Mrs Lyons question 'Doesn't one get piles when one is pregnant?' likely to cause some laughter at a performance?

Understanding performance

Look at Russell's Production Note before the start of the play on page 7.

- What are the advantages of having no scene changes? Think about the passage of time and the different locations where the action takes place.

- Adult actors are meant to play the children in this scene. How would that affect the way the acting works? Look closely at specific sections, such as the conversation between Mickey and Edward.

- The actor playing the narrator, as well as playing this role, will double up in other roles. What effect will this have?

- Many parts of this scene require 'silent tableaux' (acting without speech), such as the opening sequence after the lights come up, where the ending of the play is re-enacted. How effective is this kind of technique?

- There is tremendous pace and movement on stage in this sequence. How does Russell achieve this?

Tasks

Personal response: writing

1   Imagine a situation where two young children meet for the first time. Write a short scene that makes this come to life. Try to use the language and interests of children to make the scene effective.

2   Write a diary entry that covers a typical day in the busy life of Mrs Johnstone. Try and bring out aspects of her life that are found in the play.

3   What is the importance of money in this opening scene? How does this theme enable Russell to produce interesting drama?

    You should write about:

    a) who has money and who needs money

    b) what deals are made

    c) whether money leads to happiness.

4   What are your feelings about Mrs Lyons in this scene? Look at:

a) her actions

b) her words

c) her attitudes to others.

5   How does Russell show the divisions in society?

You should write about:

a) the way society is divided

b) the effects of poverty and wealth

c) the relationships Russell presents.

Practical activities

Individually or in pairs

6   Design a poster for *Blood Brothers*, bringing out what you think are the most important features.

7   Write a letter from Mrs Johnstone to Mrs Lyons explaining that you have changed your mind about the agreement to give one of your twins away.

8   Research the background to the play using the following website as a start:

http://www.student.nada.kth.se/~d97-ask/blood/blood.htm

In groups

9   Discuss Mrs Lyons 'sacking' of Mrs Johnstone from her cleaning job. What are your views of her behaviour and is there any other action she can take?

10   Perform the play in class:

a) allocate parts

b) decide what to do with the verse (sing or speak?)

c) decide on the style of acting

d) learn to play children.

Useful notes

overture	opening music – remember, this is a musical play
narrator	the character telling the story, and providing comments as the play develops

'do'	a party, an example of Russell's use of slang and dialect
gynaecologist	a doctor who specialises in women's reproductive systems
Welfare	slang for Social Services who are concerned about the well-being of the Johnstone family, with so many mouths to feed
George Henry Lee	a department store in Liverpool, catering for middle-class customers
effin' and blindin'	swearing
piles	an uncomfortable medical condition of the anus
pact	a contract
catalogue man	poorer families would often buy goods on credit from a catalogue
finance man	Mrs Johnstone has borrowed money to purchase goods
the park	to indicate a better area of the city, with 'big houses'
super	Edward's slang is very much that of the middle classes
pissed off	an example of Mickey's slang which is more 'common'
Eddie	Mickey renames Edward indicating a closer relationship

A Classic American Drama: *A View from the Bridge* by Arthur Miller

Background and context

Arthur Miller was born in 1915 in New York and experienced poverty in the 1930s after his father's business collapsed. However, Miller was able to save enough money to go to the University of Michigan, where he first became involved in the theatre.

He is one of the most famous living playwrights in the United States. He has been writing plays since the late 1940s and has had many successes, the most famous of which is *Death of a Salesman*. Miller's plays explore society to uncover the kinds of difficulties and problems that make interesting drama. His plays are always very well constructed with strong characters and stories. They often use the stage in a very interesting way. He uses ordinary language and settings and chooses to write plays about ordinary people. *A View from the Bridge* is an excellent example of Miller's drama.

A View from the Bridge

Act 1

[They enter the apartment. The lights in the living-room have risen and BEATRICE *is there. She looks past the sobbing* CATHERINE *at* EDDIE, *who in the presence of his wife, makes an awkward gesture of eroded command, indicating* CATHERINE.]

EDDIE: Why don't you straighten her out?

BEATRICE *[inwardly angered at his flowing emotion, which in itself alarms her]:* When are you going to leave her alone?

EDDIE: B., the guy is no good!

BEATRICE *[suddenly, with open fright and fury]:* You going to leave her alone? Or you gonna drive me crazy? *[He turns, striving to retain his dignity, but nevertheless in guilt walks out of the house, into the street and away.* CATHERINE *starts into a bedroom.]* Listen, Catherine. *[*CATHERINE *halts, turns to her sheepishly.]* What are you going to do with yourself?

CATHERINE: I don't know.

BEATRICE: Don't tell me you don't know; you're not a baby any more, what are you going to do with yourself?

CATHERINE: He won't listen to me.

BEATRICE: I don't understand this. He's not your father, Catherine. I don't understand what's going on here.

CATHERINE [*as one who herself is trying to rationalize a buried impulse*]: What am I going to do, just kick him in the face with it?

BEATRICE: Look, honey, you wanna get married, or don't you wanna get married? What are you worried about, Katie?

CATHERINE [*quietly trembling*]: I don't know B. It just seems wrong if he's against it so much.

BEATRICE [*never losing her aroused alarm*]: Sit down, honey, I want to tell you something. Here, sit down. Was there ever any fella he liked for you? There wasn't, was there?

CATHERINE: But he says Rodolpho's just after his papers.

BEATRICE: Look, he'll say anything. What does he care what he says? If it was a prince came here for you it would be no different. You know that, don't you?

CATHERINE: Yeah, I guess.

BEATRICE: So what does that mean?

CATHERINE [*slowly turns her head to* BEATRICE]: What?

BEATRICE: It means you gotta be your own self more. You still think you're a little girl, honey. But nobody else can make up your mind for you any more, you understand? You gotta give him to understand that he can't give you orders no more.

CATHERINE: Yeah, but how am I going to do that? He thinks I'm a baby.

BEATRICE: Because *you* think you're a baby. I told you fifty times already, you can't act the way you act. You still walk around in front of him in your slip —

CATHERINE: Well I forgot.

BEATRICE: Well you can't do it. Or like you sit on the edge of the bathtub talkin' to him when he's shavin' in his underwear.

CATHERINE: When'd I do that?

BEATRICE: I seen you in there this morning.

CATHERINE: Oh... well, I wanted to tell him something and I —

BEATRICE: I know, honey. But if you act like a baby and he be treatin' you like a baby. Like when he comes home sometimes you throw yourself at him like when you was twelve years old.

CATHERINE: Well I like to see him and I'm happy so I —

BEATRICE: Look, I'm not tellin' you what to do honey, but —

CATHERINE: No, you could tell me, B.! Gee, I'm all mixed up. See, I — He looks so sad now and it hurts me.

BEATRICE: Well look, Katie, if it's goin' to hurt you so much you're gonna end up an old maid here.

CATHERINE: No!

BEATRICE: I'm tellin' you, I'm not makin' a joke. I tried to tell you a couple of times in the last year or so. That's why I was so happy you were going to go out and get work, you wouldn't be here so much, you'd be a little more independent. I mean it. It's wonderful for a whole family to love each other, but you're a grown woman and you're in the same house with a grown man. So you'll act different now, heh?

CATHERINE: Yeah, I will. I'll remember.

BEATRICE: Because it ain't only up to him, Katie, you understand? I told him the same thing already.

CATHERINE [*quickly*]: What?

BEATRICE: That he should let you go. But, you see, if only I tell him, he thinks I'm just bawlin' him out, or maybe I'm jealous or somethin', you know?

CATHERINE [*astonished*]: He said you was jealous?

BEATRICE: No, I'm just sayin' maybe that's what he thinks. [*She reaches over to* CATHERINE'S *hand; with a strained smile*] You think I'm jealous of you, honey?

CATHERINE: No! It's the first I thought of it..

BEATRICE [*with a quiet sad laugh*]: Well you should have thought of it before ... but I'm not. We'll be all right. Just give him to understand; you don't have to fight, you're just — You're a woman, that's all, and you got a nice boy, and now the time came when you said good-bye. All right?

CATHERINE [*strangely moved at the prospect*]: All right… If I can.

BEATRICE: Honey… you gotta.

[CATHERINE, *sensing now an imperious demand, turns with some fear, with a discovery, to* BEATRICE. *She is at the edge of tears, as though a familiar world had shattered.*]

CATHERINE: Okay.

Eddie (Michael Gambon), Beatrice (Elizabeth Bell), and Catherine, played by Susan Sylvester, at the National Theatre, 1987.

[Lights out on them and up on ALFIERI, *seated behind his desk.]*

ALFIERI: It was at this time that he first came to me. I had represented his father in an accident case some years before, and I was acquainted with the family in a casual way. I remember him now as he walked through my doorway —

[Enter EDDIE *down right ramp.]*

His eyes were like tunnels; my first thought was that he had committed a crime, [EDDIE *sits beside the desk, cap in hand, looking out.]* but soon I saw it was only a passion that had moved into his body, like a stranger. [ALFIERI *pauses, looks down at his desk, then to* EDDIE *as though he were continuing a conversation with him.]* I don't quite understand what I can do for you.

Is there a question of law somewhere?

EDDIE: That's what I want to ask you.

ALFIERI: Because there's nothing illegal about a girl falling in love with an immigrant.

EDDIE: Yeah, but what about it if the only reason for it is to get his papers?

ALFIERI: First of all you don't know that.

EDDIE: I see it in his eyes; he's laughin' at her and he's laughin' at me…

ALFIERI: Eddie, I'm a lawyer. I can only deal in what's provable. You understand that, don't you? Can you prove that?

EDDIE: *I know what's in his mind, Mr Alfieri!*

ALFIERI: Eddie, even if you could prove that —

EDDIE: Listen… will you listen to me a minute? My father always said you was a smart man. I want you to listen to me.

ALFIERI: I'm only a lawyer, Eddie.

EDDIE: Will you listen a minute? I'm talkin' about the law. Lemme just bring out what I mean. A man, which be comes into the country illegal, don't it stand to reason he's gonna take every penny and put it in the sock? Because they don't know from one day to another, right?

ALFIERI: All right.

EDDIE; He's spendin'. Records he buys now. Shoes. Jackets. Y'understand me? This guy ain't worried. This guy is *here*. So it must be that he's got it all laid out in his mind already — he's stayin'. Right?

ALFIERI: Well? What about it?

EDDIE: All right. *[He glances at* ALFIERI, *then down to the floor.]*

I'm talking to you confidential, ain't I?

ALFIERI: Certainly.

EDDIE: I mean it don't go no place but here. Because I don't like to say this about anybody. Even my wife I didn't exactly say this.

ALFIERI: What is it?

EDDIE *[takes a breath and glances briefly over each shoulder]:* The guy ain't right, Mr Alfieri.

ALFIERI: What do you mean?

EDDIE: I mean he ain't right.

ALFIBRI: I don't get you.

EDDIE *[shifts to another position in the chair]:* D'ja ever get a look at him?

ALFIERI: Not that I know of, no.

EDDIE: He's a blond guy. Like … platinum. You know what I mean?

ALFIERI: No.

EDDIE: I mean if you dose the paper fast — you could blow him over.

ALFIERI: Well that doesn't mean —

EDDIE: Wait a minute, I'm tellin' you sump'm. He sings, see. Which is I mean it's all right, but sometimes he hits a note, see. I turn around. I mean — high. You know what I mean?

ALFIERI: Well, that's a tenor.

EDDIE: I know a tenor, Mr Alfieri. This ain't no tenor. I mean if you came in the house and you didn't know who was singin', you wouldn't be lookin' for him you be lookin' for her.

ALFIERI: Yes, but that's not —

EDDIE: I'm tellin' you sump'm, wait a minute. Please, Mr Alfieri. I'm tryin' to bring out my thoughts here. Couple of nights ago my niece brings out a dress which it's too small for her, because she shot up like a light this last year. He takes the dress, lays it on the table, he cuts it up; one-two-three, he makes a new dress. I mean he looked so sweet there, like an angel — you could kiss him he was so sweet.

ALFIERI: Now look, Eddie —

EDDIE: Mr Alfieri, they're laughin' at him on the piers. I'm ashamed. Paper Doll they call him. Blondie now. His brother thinks it's because he's got a sense of humour, see — which he's got — but that ain't what they're laughin'. Which they're not goin' to come out with it because they know he's my relative, which they have to see me if they make a crack, y'know? But I know what they're laughin' at, and when I think of that guy layin' his hands on her I could — I mean it's eatin' me out, Mr Alfieri, because I struggled for that girl. And now he comes in my house and —

ALFIERI: Eddie, look — I have my own children. I understand you. But the law is very specific. The law does not…

EDDIE [with a fuller flow of indignation]: You mean to tell me that there's no law that a guy which he ain't right can go to work and marry a girl and —?

ALFIERI: You have no recourse in the law, Eddie…

EDDIE: Yeah, but if he ain't right, Mr Alfieri, you mean to tell me —

ALFIERI: There is nothing you can do, Eddie, believe me.

EDDIE: Nothin'.

ALPIERI: Nothing at all. There's only one legal question here.

EDDIE: What?

ALFIERI: The manner in which they entered the country. But I don't think you want to do anything about that, do you?

EDDIE: You mean —?

ALFIERI: Well, they entered illegally.

EDDIE: Oh, Jesus, no, I wouldn't do nothin' about that, I mean —

ALFIERI: All right, then, let me talk now, eh?

EDDIE: Mr Alfieri, I can't believe what you tell me. I mean there must be some kinda law which —

ALFIERI: Eddie, I want you to listen to me. [Pause.] You know, sometimes God mixes up the people. We all love somebody, the wife; the kids — every man's got somebody that he loves, heh? But sometimes… there's too much. You know? There's too much, and it goes where it mustn't. A man works hard, he brings up a child, sometimes it's a niece, sometimes even a daughter, and he never realizes it, but through the years — there is too much love for the daughter, there is too much love for the niece. Do you understand what I'm saying to you?

EDDIE [*sardonically*]: What do you mean, I shouldn't look out for her good?

ALFIERI: Yes, but those things have to end, Eddie, that's all.

The child has to grow up and go away, and the man has to learn to forget. Because after all, Eddie — what other way can it end? [*Pause.*] Let her go. That's my advice. You did your job, now it's her life; wish her luck, and let her go. [*Pause.*] Will you do that? Because there's no law, Eddie; make up your mind to it; the law is not interested in this.

EDDIE: You mean to tell me, even if he's a punk? If he's —

ALFIERI: There's nothing you can do.

[EDDIE *stands.*]

EDDIE: Well, all right, thanks. Thanks very much.

ALFIERI: What are you going to do?

EDDIE [*with a helpless but ironic gesture*]: What can I do? I'm a patsy, what can a patsy do? I worked like a dog twenty years so a punk could have her, so that's what I done. I mean, in the worst times, in the worst, when there wasn't a ship comin' in the harbour, I didn't stand around lookin' for relief — I hustled. When there was empty piers in Brooklyn I went to Hoboken, Staten Island, the West Side, Jersey all over — because I made a promise. I took out of my own mouth to give to her. I took out of my wife's mouth. I walked hungry plenty days in this city! [*It begins to break through.*] And now I gotta sit in my own house and look at a son-of-a-bitch punk like that — which he came out of nowhere! I give him my house to sleep! I take the blankets off my bed for him, and he takes and puts his dirty filthy hands on her like a goddam thief!

ALFIERI [*rising*]: But, Eddie, she's a woman now.

EDDIE: He's stealing her from me!

ALFIERI: She wants to get married, Eddie. She can't marry you, can she?

EDDIE [*furiously*]: What're you talkin' about, marry me! I don't know what the hell you're talkin' about!

[*Pause.*]

ALFIERI: I gave you my advice, Eddie. That's it.

[EDDIE *gathers himself. A pause.*]

EDDIE: Well, thanks. Thanks very much. It just — it's breakin' my heart, y'know. I —

ALFIERI: I understand. Put it out of your mind. Can you do that?

EDDIE: I'm — [*He feels the threat of sobs, and with a helpless wave*] I'll see you around. [*He goes out up the right ramp.*]

ALFIERI [*sits on desk*]: There are times when you want to spread an alarm, but nothing has happened. I knew, I knew then and there — I could have finished the whole story that afternoon. It wasn't as though there was a mystery to unravel. I could see every step coming, step after step, like a dark figure walking down a hall towards a certain door. I knew where he was heading for, I knew where he was going to end. And I sat here many afternoons asking myself why, being an intelligent man, I was so powerless to stop it. I even went to a certain old lady in the neighbourhood, a very wise old woman, and I told her, and she only nodded, and said, 'Pray for him...' And so I — waited here.

[*As lights go out on* ALFIERI, *they rise in the apartment where all are finishing dinner.* BEATRICE *and* CATHERINE *are clearing the table.*]

CATHERINE: You know where they went?

BEATRICE: Where?

CATHERINE: They went to Africa once. On a fishing boat.

[EDDIE *glances at her.*] It's true, Eddie.

[BEATRICE *exits into the kitchen with dishes.*]

EDDIE: I didn't say nothin'. *[He goes to his rocker, picks up a newspaper]*

CATHERINE: And I was never even in Staten Island.

EDDIE *[sitting with the paper]:* You didn't miss nothin'.

[Pause. CATHERINE takes dished out.] How long that take you, Marco — to get to Africa?

MARCO *[rising]:* Oh... two days. We go all over.

RODOLPHO *[rising]:* Once we went to Yugoslavia.

EDDIE *[to MARCO]:* They pay all right on them boats?

[BEATRICE *enters. She and* RODOLPHO *stack the remaining dishes.*]

MARCO: If they catch fish they pay all right. *[Sits on a stool.]*

RODOLPHO: They're family boats, though. And nobody in our family owned one. So we only worked when one of the families was sick.

BEATRICE: Y'know, Marco, what I don't understand — there's an ocean full of fish and yiz are all starvin'.

EDDIE: They gotta have boats, nets, you need money.

[CATHERINE *enters.*]

BEATRICE: Yeah, but couldn't they like fish from the beach? You see them down Coney Island —

MARCO: Sardines.

EDDIE: Sure. *[Laughing]* How you gonna catch sardines on a hook?

BEATRICE: Oh, I didn't know they're sardines. *[To* CATHERINE] They're sardines!

CATHERINE: Yeah, they follow them all over the ocean, Africa, Yugoslavia... *[She sits and begins, to look through a movie magazine.* RODOLPHO *joins her.]*

BEATRICE *[to EDDIE]:* It's funny, y'know. You never think of it, that sardines are swimming in the ocean! *[She exits to kitchen with dishes.]*

CATHERINE: I know. It's like oranges and lemons on a tree. *[To* EDDIE] I mean you ever think of oranges and lemons on a tree?

EDDIE: Yeah, I know. It's funny. *[To* MARCO] I heard that they paint the oranges to make them look orange.

[BEATRICE *enters.*]

MARCO *[He has been reading a letter]:* Paint?

EDDIE: Yeah, I heard that they grow like green.

MARCO: No, in Italy the oranges are orange.

RODOLPHO: Lemons are green.

EDDIE *[resenting his instruction]:* I know lemons are green, for Christ's sake, you see them in the store they're green sometimes. I said oranges they paint, I didn't say nothin' about lemons.

BEATRICE *[sitting; diverting their attention]:* Your wife is gettin' the money all right, Marco?

MARCO: Oh, yes. She bought medicine for my boy.

BEATRICE: That's wonderful. You feel better, heh?

MARCO: Oh, yes! But I'm lonesome.

BEATRICE: I just hope you ain't gonna do like some of them around here. They're here twenty-five years, some men, and they didn't get enough together to go back twice.

MARCO: Oh, I know. We have many families in our town, the children never saw the father. But I will go home. Three, four years, I think.

BEATRICE: Maybe you should keep more here. Because maybe she thinks it comes so easy you'll never get ahead of yourself.

MARCO: Oh, no, she saves. I send everything. My wife is very lonesome. *[He smiles shyly.]*

BEATRICE: She must be nice. She pretty? I bet, heh?

MARCO *[blushing]:* No, but she understand everything.

RODOLPHO: Oh, he's got a clever wife!

EDDIE: I betcha there's plenty surprises sometimes when those guys get back there heh?

MARCO: Surprises?

EDDIE *[laughing]:* I mean, you know — they count the kids and there's a couple extra than when they left?

MARCO: No — no… The women wait, Eddie. Most Most. Very few surprises.

RODOLPHO: It's more strict in our town. [EDDIE *looks at him now.]* It's not so free.

EDDIE *[rises, paces up and down]:* It ain't so free here either, Rodolpho, like you think. I seen greenhorns sometimes get in trouble that way they think just because a girl don't go around with a shawl over her head that she ain't strict, y'know? Girl don't have to wear black dress to be strict. Know what I mean?

RODOLPHO: Well, I always have respect —

EDDIE: I know, but in your town you wouldn't just drag off some girl without permission, I mean. *[He turns.]* You know what I mean, Marco? It ain't that much different, here.

MARCO *[cautiously]:* Yes.

BEATRICE: Well, he didn't exactly drag her off though, Eddie.

EDDIE: I know, but I seen some of them get the wrong idea sometimes. *[To* RODOLPHO]* I mean it might be a little more free here but it's just as strict.

RODOLPHO: I have respect for her, Eddie. I do anything wrong?

EDDIE: Look, kid, I ain't her father, I'm only her uncle —

BEATRICE: Well then, be an uncle then. [EDDIE *looks at her, aware of her criticizing force.]* I mean.

MARCO: No, Beatrice, if he does wrong you must tell him. *[To* EDDIE]* What does he do wrong?

EDDIE: Well, Marco, till he came here she was never out on the street twelve o'clock at night.

MARCO *[to* RODOLPHO]:* You come home early now.

BEATRICE *[to* CATHERINE]:* Well, you said the movie ended late, didn't you?

CATHERINE: Yeah.

BEATRICE: Well, tell him, honey. *[To* EDDIE]* The movie ended late.

EDDIE: Look, B., I'm just sayin' — he thinks she always stayed out like that.

MARCO: You come home early now, Rodolpho.

RODOLPHO *[embarrassed]:* All right, sure. But I can't stay in the house all the time, Eddie.

EDDIE: Look, kid, I'm not only talkin' about her. The more you run around like that the more chance you're takin'. *[To* BEATRICE*]* I mean suppose he gets hit by a car or something. *[To* MARCO*]* Where's his papers, who is he? Know what I mean?

BEATRICE: Yeah, but who is he in the daytime, though? It's the same chance in the daytime.

EDDIE *[holding back a voice full of anger]*: Yeah, but he don't have to go lookin' for it, Beatrice. If he's here to work, then he should work; if he's here for a good time then he could fool around! *[To* MARCO*]* But I understood, Marco, that you was both comin' to make a livin' for your family. You understand me, don't you, Marco? *[He goes to his rocker.]*

MARCO: I beg your pardon, Eddie.

EDDIE: I mean, that's what I understood in the first place, see.

MARCO: Yes. That's why we came.

EDDIE *[sits on his rocker]:* Well, that's all I'm askin'.

*[*EDDIE *reads his paper. There is a pause, an awkwardness. Now* CATHERINE *gets up and puts a record on the phonograph – Paper Doll.]*

CATHERINE *[flushed with revolt]:* You wanna dance, Rodolpho? *[*EDDIE *freezes.]*

RODOLPHO *[in deference to* EDDIE*]:* No, I — I'm tired.

BEATRICE: Go ahead, dance, Rodolpho.

CATHERINE: Ah, come on. They got a beautiful quartet, these guys. Come.

[She has taken his hand and he stiffly rises, feeling EDDIE'S *eyes on his back, and they dance.]*

EDDIE *[to* CATHERINE*]:* What's that, a new record?

CATHERINE: It's the same one. We bought it the other day.

BEATRICE *[to* EDDIE*]:* They only bought three records. *[She watches them dance;* EDDIE *turns his head away.* MARCO *just sits there, waiting. Now* BEATRICE *turns to* EDDIE.*]* Must be nice to go all over in one of them fishin' boats. I would like that myself. See all them other countries?

EDDIE: Yeah.

BEATRICE *[to* MARCO*]:* But the women don't go along, I bet.

MARCO: No, not on the boats. Hard work.

BEATRICE: What're you got, a regular kitchen and everything?

MARCO: Yes, we eat very good on the boats — especially when Rodolpho comes along; everybody gets fat.

BEATRICE: Oh, he cooks?

MARCO: Sure, very good cook. Rice, pasta, fish, everything.

*[*EDDIE *lowers his paper.]*

EDDIE: He's a cook, too! *[Looking at* RODOLPHO*]* He sings, he cooks...

*[*RODOLPHO *smiles thankfully.]*

BEATRICE: Well it's good, he could always make a living.

EDDIE: It's wonderful. He sings, he cooks, he could make dresses...

CATHERINE: They get some high pay, them guys. The head chefs in all the big hotels are men. You read about them.

EDDIE: That's what I'm sayin'.

*[*CATHERINE *and* RODOLPHO *continue dancing.]*

CATHERINE: Yeah, well, I mean.

Eddie, played by Michael Gambon, Aldwych Theatre, 1987.

EDDIE *[to* BEATRICE]: He's lucky, believe me. *[Slight pause. He looks away, then back to* BEATRICE.] That's why the water-front is no place for him. *[They stop dancing.* RODOLPHO *turns off phonograph.]* I mean like me — I can't cook, I can't sing, I can't make dresses, so I'm on the waterfront. But if I could cook, if I could sing, if I could make dresses, I wouldn't be on the water-front. *[He has been unconsciously twisting the newspaper into a tight roll. They are all regarding him now; he senses he is exposing the issue and he is driven on.]* I would be someplace else. I would be like in a dress store. *[He has bent the rolled paper and it suddenly tears in two. He suddenly gets up and pulls his pants up over his belly and goes to* MARCO.] What do you say, Marco, we go to the bouts next Saturday night. You never seen a fight, did you?

MARCO *[uneasily]:* Only in the moving pictures

EDDIE *[going to* RODOLPHO]: I'll treat yiz. What do you say, Danish? You wanna come along? I'll buy the tickets.

RODOLPHO: Sure. I like to go.

CATHERINE *[goes to* EDDIE; *nervously happy now]:* I'll make some coffee, all right?

EDDIE: Go ahead, make some! Make it nice and strong. *[Mystified, she smiles and exits to kitchen. He is weirdly elated, rubbing his fists into his palms. He strides to* MARCO.] You wait, Marco, you see some real fights here. You ever do any boxing?

MARCO: No, I never.

EDDIE *[to* RODOLPHO]: Betcha you have done some, heh?

RODOLPHO: No.

EDDIE: Well, come on, I'll teach you.

BEATRICE: What's he got to learn that for?

EDDIE: Ya can't tell, one a these days somebody's liable to step on his foot or sump'n. Come on, Rodolpho, I show you a couple of passes. *[He stands below table.]*

BEATRICE: Go ahead, Rodolpho. He's a good boxer, he could teach you.

RODOLPHO *[embarrassed]:* Well, I don't know how to — *[He moves down to* EDDIE.]

EDDIE: Just put your hands up. Like this, see? That's right. That's very good, keep your left up, because you lead with the left, see, like this. *[He gently moves his left into* RODOLPHO'S *face.]* See? Now what you gotta do is you gotta block me, so when I come in like that you — [RODOLPHO *parries his left.]* Hey, that's very good! [RODOLPHO *laughs.]* All right, now come into me. Come on.

RODOLPHO: I don't want to hit you Eddie.

EDDIE: Don't pity me, come on. Throw it, I'll show you how to block it. [RODOLPHO *jabs at him, laughing. The others join.]* 'at's it. Come on again. For the jaw right here. [RODOLPHO *jabs with more assurance.]* Very good!

BEATRICE *[to* MARCO]: He's very good!

[EDDIE *crosses directly upstage of* RODOLPHO.]

EDDIE: Sure, he's great! Come on, kid, put sump'n behind it, you can't hurt me.

[RODOLPHO, *more seriously, jabs at* EDDIE's *jaw and grazes it.]* Attaboy.

[CATHERINE *comes from the kitchen, watches.]*

Now I'm gonna hit you, so block me, see?

CATHERINE *[with beginning alarm]:* What are they doin'?

[They are lightly boxing now.]

BEATRICE *[she senses only the comradeship in it now]:* He's teachin' him; he's very good!

EDDIE: Sure, he's terrific! Look at him go! [RODOLPHO *lands a blow.*] 'at's it! Now, watch out, here I come, Danish! *[He feints with his left hand and lands with his right. It mildly staggers* RODOLPHO. MARCO *rises.]*

CATHERINE *[rushing to* RODOLPHO]: Eddie!

EDDIE: Why? I didn't hurt him. Did I hurt you, kid? *[He rubs the back of his hand across his mouth.]*

RODOLPHO: No, no, he didn't hurt me. [To EDDIE *with a certain gleam and a smile]* I was only surprised.

BEATRICE *[pulling* EDDIE *down into the rocker]:* That's enough, Eddie; he did pretty good, though.

EDDIE: Yeah. *[Rubbing his fists together]* He could be very good, Marco. I'll teach him again.

[MARCO *nods at him dubiously.]*

RODOLPHO: Dance, Catherine. Come.

[He takes her hand; they go to the phonograph and start it. It plays Paper Doll.

RODOLPHO *takes her in his arms. They dance.* EDDIE *in thought sits in his chair, and* MARCO *takes a chair, places it in front of* EDDIE, *and looks down at it.* BEATRICE *and* EDDIE *watch him.]*

MARCO: Can you lift this chair?

EDDIE: What do you mean?

MARCO: From here. *[He gets on one knee with one hand behind his back, and grasps the bottom of one of the chair legs but does not raise it.]*

EDDIE: Sure, why not? *[He comes to the chair, kneels, grasps the leg, raises the chair one inch, but it leans over to the floor]* Gee, that's hard, I never knew that. *[He tries again, and again fails.]* It's on an angle, that's why, heh?

MARCO: Here.

[He kneels, grasps, and with strain slowly raises the chair higher and higher, getting to his fret now. RODOLPHO *and* CATHERINE *have stopped dancing as* MARCO *raises the chair over his head.*

MARCO *is face to face with* EDDIE, *a strained tension gripping his eyes and jaw, his neck stiffens the chair raised like a weapon over* EDDIE'S *head — and he transforms what might appear like a glare of warning into a smile of triumph, and* EDDIE'S *grin vanishes as he absorbs his look.]*

Understanding action and structure

The play is set among the Italian community in New York's 'Red Hook', a slum area on the seaward side, under Brooklyn Bridge. The events of the play focus closely on the lives of the members of the Carbone household: Eddie Carbone, his wife Beatrice and his niece Catherine. This cosy family life is disturbed by the arrival of Beatrice's cousins, Marco and Rodolpho, who have illegally entered the United States to raise money for their family back home in Italy. As the play progresses, Catherine strikes up a relationship with Rodolpho and Eddie's reactions to this provide most of the tension and interest in the play. In particular, Eddie finds himself in conflict with Marco, a feature that is evident in our extract.

• Why is Beatrice angry in the opening to the excerpt and what is Eddie's response?

• What is the advice that Beatrice gives to Catherine here?

Eddie speaks to the lawyer Alfieri in the hope of doing something about Rodolpho and Catherine.

• What are the two main complaints that Eddie makes about Rodolpho as he talks to Alfieri?

• When Alfieri is left alone he speaks directly to the audience. What does he say?

In the final section of the extract, the main characters are all together. The problems that Eddie has with regard to Rodolpho and Catherine remain hidden, but boiling away under the surface. This is shown by the tension between the characters.

• How is the conflict between Eddie and Rodolpho shown in this scene?

• How is the conflict between Eddie and Marco shown?

The play is brilliantly structured over two acts and the conflict between Eddie and Marco is matched in the second act. Eddie betrays Marco and Rodolpho to the Immigration Office, and the consequences of this act lead to his death.

Understanding character

The main characters are:

Eddie

Beatrice

Catherine

Marco

Rodolpho.

In this extract we see Eddie's character under a great deal of strain and he seems very troubled. What does the following excerpt tell us about his feelings for Catherine?

> EDDIE: …I give him my house to sleep! I take the blankets off my bed for him, and he takes and puts his dirty filthy hands on her like a goddam thief!
>
> ALFIERI [*rising*]: But, Eddie, she's a woman now.
>
> EDDIE: He's stealing her from me!
>
> ALFIERI: She wants to get married, Eddie. She can't marry you, can she?
>
> EDDIE [*furiously*]: What're you talkin' about, marry me! I don't know what the hell you're talkin' about!
>
> [*Pause*]

- Beatrice is concerned more about Catherine's future than anything else. What evidence can you find in the excerpt to show Beatrice's care for Catherine?

Understanding themes

The key themes of this play are family loyalty, jealousy, growing up and betrayal.

Family loyalty

Catherine is torn between loyalty to the family she has been brought up in and her new loyalty to Rodolpho. Beatrice, on the other hand, is torn between loyalty to her husband and her desire to see her niece Catherine happy in her life.

Look at the extract where Beatrice advises Catherine to break away from her family on page 33.

- What do we learn of each character's feelings at this point?

Other aspects of family loyalty are shown in the character of Marco who has come to the United States to provide for his family in Italy. He is also protective of Rodolpho.

Jealousy

Eddie's jealousy is a serious threat to everyone around him. He has developed very strong feelings for his niece but is unable to see that they might be more than just protective. Eddie's jealousy also comes through in his attitude to Rodolpho.

- Look again at the ending of the extract. Find examples of Eddie's attitude to Rodolpho.

Growing up

Catherine has reached an age where she must take responsibility for herself. Also, if she wants to get on well with her family she needs to get away from Eddie. In Miller's drama the relationship between the generations is very important and another of his well-known plays *Death of a Salesman* is a wonderful examination of this aspect of life.

Betrayal

At the end of the play, Eddie betrays Marco and Rodolpho by informing on them to the Immigration Office.

Look at the following excerpt:

> ALFIERI: There is nothing you can do, Eddie, believe me.
> EDDIE: Nothin'.
> ALPIERI: Nothing at all. There's only one legal question here.
> EDDIE: What?
> ALFIERI: The manner in which they entered the country. But I don't think you want to do anything about that, do you?
> EDDIE: You mean —?
> ALFIERI: Well, they entered illegally.
> EDDIE: Oh, Jesus, no, I wouldn't do nothin' about that, I mean —

- How is the theme of betrayal prepared for in the excerpt?

Understanding dramatic devices

Arthur Miller has a reputation for knowing how to move an audience through the clever use of dramatic devices such as language, action and conflict.

Language

The story of *A View from the Bridge* is set amongst the Italian community of New York. Miller uses language that clearly reflects the language that this tough, working-class community uses.

Look at the following brief interaction:

> BEATRICE: Y'know, Marco, what I don't understand — there's an ocean full of fish and yiz are all starvin'.
> EDDIE: They gotta have boats, nets, you need money.
> [CATHERINE *enters.*]
> BEATRICE: Yeah, but couldn't they like fish from the beach? You see them down Coney Island —

- Write this out in standard English and see what differences there are. Now look at the rest of the excerpt, paying attention to the language.

Action

Look at the section where Eddie and Rodolpho spar with each other. This mock boxing match very quickly becomes quite serious and Miller wants to let Marco show that he is also physically capable of dealing with Eddie if he needs to.

- What action does Marco take?

Conflict

Conflict is one of the key dramatic devices that any dramatist will use. It is often said that without conflict there is no drama. In this play there is conflict between Eddie and Beatrice, Eddie and Catherine, Eddie and Rodolpho and Eddie and Marco.

- How is the conflict between Eddie and Marco shown in this excerpt?

Understanding performance

Miller uses a set that involves three main areas of action: the Carbone apartment, Alfieri's office, and the street.

Look at the following extract:

> BEATRICE: …You're a woman, that's all, and you got a nice boy, and now the time came when you said good-bye. All right?
> CATHERINE [*strangely moved at the prospect*]: All right… If I can.
> BEATRICE: Honey… you gotta.
> [CATHERINE, *sensing now an imperious demand, turns with some fear, with a discovery, to* BEATRICE. *She is at the edge of tears, as though a familiar world had shattered.*]
> CATHERINE: Okay.
> [*Lights out on them and up on* ALFIERI, *seated behind his desk.*]
> ALFIERI: It was at this time that he first came to me. I had represented his father in an accident case some years before…

- How effective do you think the change from one location to another is in this extract? How does what Beatrice and Catherine are talking about relate to what Eddie and Alfieri are discussing?

The actor playing Eddie in *A View from the Bridge* has a huge task in creating a character who is both unpleasant and also sympathetic to an audience. In this extract, Eddie's anger is very much to the fore.

- Look again at the scene with Alfieri. Can you find the moments in the scene where Eddie's anger increases? Why does his anger increase at these moments?

Tasks

Personal response: writing

1   Write a scene in which a mother goes to speak to a priest about the fact that her son seems to be throwing himself away on a worthless girl. (This is a role-reversal, in a sense, of the Eddie/Alfieri scene.)

2   What is your response to Eddie in this extract?

You should write about:

a) his relationship with Beatrice

b) his attitude to Catherine

c) how he treats Marco and Rodolpho.

3   Look closely at the conversation between Beatrice and Catherine. What do you think about the situation in the Carbone household?

You should write about:

a) Beatrice's advice to Catherine

b) Catherine's feelings for Eddie.

Practical activities

Individually or in pairs

4   Write a continuation scene between Eddie, Marco and Rodolpho in which they meet on the street. Try to use some of the ideas and language that are found in this extract and also bring out the conflict between the characters.

Look at the following sites to help in your research:

http://www.kirjasto.sci.fi/amiller.htm
http://metalab.unc.edu/miller/

In groups or class

5   Allocate parts and act out the extract.

6   After acting out the extract, rehearse the final section and freeze the action at the very end of the extract. Now ask the actors to stay in character and interview each character in turn, asking questions about their feelings and attitudes at that point. (This sort of exercise is known sometimes as 'tableau talkback'.)

Useful notes

Or you gonna drive me crazy?	make me angry, frustrated. Notice the use of informal American speech
rationalize a buried impulse	trying to make sense of buried feelings and ideas
imperious demand	an instruction that must be followed
Dja	Did you (i.e. did ya, American speech)
put it in the sock	save the money at home, without using a bank
like an angel	Eddie seems to have rather confused feelings here
punk	a worthless person, usually criminal
patsy	the victim of a confidence trick
surprises	Eddie is getting close to being rude here
he sings, he cooks	there is a suggestion about Rodolpho here

Women Writers: *True Dare Kiss* by Debbie Horsfield

Background and context

Debbie Horsfield was born in Manchester and has been a successful writer since the mid 1980s. Her first plays were premiered at the Liverpool Playhouse Theatre but she has since gone on to work in television. Her recent television work has been very popular with such triumphs as *Making Out* and *Born To Run*. These have gained her the reputation of someone who looks closely at women's lives today, especially the lives of working-class women. Interestingly, though, her work is not seen as anti-male in any way because she is able to create very believable and sympathetic characters of either sex.

True Dare Kiss, set in the early 1980s, takes the lives of the four characters in her early play, *Red Devils* (about the fortunes of four female Manchester United Supporters), and shows them coping with the difficulties of adult life. Horsfield takes us into the world of marriage, work, education and leisure through an interweaving saga, not unlike the style of a television soap opera.

True Dare Kiss

Extract A

Act 1

February–April 1980

As the audience arrive the sounds of Manchester United fans singing football chants can be heard. As the lights go down the chants mingle with and are finally drowned out by the sound of church bells ringing.

Outside a church in Salford. An afternoon in late February. A wedding party begins to assemble.
KEVIN (the groom) enters with JOEY (the best man) and NIDGE. BETH and NITA walk on together. ALICE (the bride) arrives with her sister JANINE. Finally PHIL walks on. She makes no attempt to speak to any of the group.

As she comes forward the wedding bells stop and the lights focus on her and the figures of
ALICE, NITA *and* BETH.

PHIL: Thanks a lot, Alice. Are y'satisfied now? Y'coulda kept yer invitation. I don't wanna come back. I put two hundred miles between me an' this dive — an' times like this it's like livin' on the doorstep.

Yeah. Okay. Once.

We divvied up. Shared things. God knows how. Classrooms… ciggies… Sat'days… spots.

Alice gets skint, so Nita coughs up. Beth's gettin' pasted so in weighs Phil. 'You hit my mate — c'mere an' say that.'

Home for tea with two black eyes an' front teeth hangin' out. 'Where y'bin, Phil? Them three again? Upstairs, you.' Thanks Beth. Thanks pal.

And four years – every week – stood with you three on the Stretford End.

(She chants:) 'Que sera sera… whatever will be will be… We're goin' to Wem-ber-lee – … que sera sera…'

United? Now? Joke, innit? Look, I don't wanna argue. Give over, will yer? It's not the same, Nita. Beth, it isn't like that now. We're not still coming back from Wembley. An' we didn't win the Cup.

The wedding bells start to ring again. From inside the church come the opening strains of the Wedding March. KEVIN, JOEY and NIDGE go off into church. ALICE, attended by JANINE and BETH, follows. NITA is about to follow when she notices PHIL is lagging behind. She goes over to her.

NITA: Y'goin' in?

PHIL: I don't know.

NITA: What y'doin' here, then?

PHIL *(without malice):* God knows.

NITA: Y'come two hundred miles, get all togged up, just so y'can stand outside?

PHIL: I don't like funerals.

NITA: Phil, it's a wedding.

PHIL: Is it?

NITA *giving up already, walks away.*

PHIL *(calling after her):* Believe it or not, Nita, I would love to be wrong.

NITA: Oh, is that right, Phil? You would love to be wrong? Well that's a new one, Phil.

NITA *walks off into church. PHIL hesitates for a moment then follows her in.*

The wedding reception.

The stage is empty. Suddenly the doors fly open and in burst NIDGE, with no shirt on, his tie round his head, leading KEVIN, JOEY, ALICE, JANINE and BETH in a conga. NITA follows. PHIL brings up the rear.

ALICE *captures NITA and takes off for a chat. PHIL is about to join BETH when KEVIN calls her. He has been drinking all afternoon and is very unsteady.*

KEVIN: Hey, Phil! *(She turns round.)* Gi's a smile, Phil? Y'gonna say congratulations?

PHIL *(determined not to be provoked):* Yeah, well done, Kevin. *(She starts to walk off.)*

KEVIN: Aw, don't be like that. *(He goes over to her.)* Y'not want us to get married then?

PHIL: What give yer that idea?

KEVIN *(putting his arm round her):* I think yer dead fit, you, y'know.

PHIL: Do yer?

KEVIN: I do, yeah. I've always fancied you.

PHIL *(gently removing his arm):* Good for you, Kevin.

KEVIN: Hey, y'know where I live, don't yer?

PHIL: Oh, don't worry Kevin — I've had it for some time. *(She starts to walk off.)*

JOEY: Hey, Phil — *(She turns back. JOEY grabs her wrist.)* Y'not gonna give the groom a good luck kiss?

NIDGE: Oh yeah, go on, Phil — give yerself a treat.

PHIL *considers for a moment then goes up to* KEVIN, *puts her arms round him and starts to kiss him.* JOEY *and* NIDGE *cheer encouragement. The kiss becomes more and more involved. Suddenly* KEVIN *starts to struggle and squeal. Finally* PHIL *releases him.*

PHIL: Now piss off, Kevin. *(She walks over to join* BETH.)

JOEY *goes over to where* KEVIN *is still clutching his mouth.*

JOEY: Aw Kevin… bit yer tongue off, did she? She must fancy yer, Kev.

JOEY, KEVIN and NIDGE sit down and break out a pack of cards.

ALICE *brings* NITA *forward to look at her wedding presents.*

NITA: Seven butter dishes? *(Looking at them.)* What d'y'want seven butter dishes for?

ALICE: I don't. I only asked for one. We don't even have butter. Kev's a Flora man. *(Counting them.)* Two plastic, two Pyrex, two stainless steel, and one Fabulous Unbreakable Melamine. *(Then, in great disgust.)* An' what d'y'think of this, then?

NITA *(pleasantly surprised):* It's a wok.

ALICE: Yeah, exactly. *What* y'supposed to do with a wok? I asked for a chip pan, Nita. What's Kev gonna have for his tea now? How'm I gonna feed him?

NITA: How d'y'mean?

Kevin and Alice's wedding, Lamda, 1988.

ALICE: Without a chip pan? What'll he eat? Y'can't always be dining out down the chippy, can yer? What do *I* look like then? *(Anticipating a response.)* Yeah, exactly — failed housewife. An' have you seen this? Look at that. Five bathmats, fifteen towels... nothing goes, of course... not one Tangerine Dream like the bathroom suite. I could scream. Oh yeah, could always repaint the bathroom, I s'pose — get a new suite put in. Trouble is, I like this one, but the towels don't go...

NITA: Alice, is everything... all right?

ALICE: Pardon?

NITA: You have done the right thing?

ALICE: Right thing?

NITA: Getting married.

ALICE: I don't know what y'mean.

NITA: To Kevin.

ALICE: Well who else would I get married to?

NITA: Look, Alice — if you ever need anything... y'know... anyone...?

ALICE: What d'y'mean? I've got Kevin. Why would I need anyone?

NITA: Y'never know...

ALICE: See Phil's not speaking to me. *(They both look round at* PHIL.*)* You tell her, Nita — bein' married's great. Y'get new clothes, y'get yer picture took — An' all them prezzies... see all that? That's my home, that is, perched up there, top of the piano. Tell Phil she dun't know what she's missing.

NITA *is on the verge of tears and pretends to have something in her eye to hide it.*

Hey, did I show yer me ring? It's not the one I asked for, but Kevin says it's got more class. I don't know where he got the money...

ALICE *is about to circulate when sounds of cheering and shouting break out. Attempts are being made to make* JOEY *give a speech.* ALICE *rejoins* KEVIN.

NIDGE *(standing up):* Okay... okay now... quiet please... *quiet* will yer?... speech... speech... best man... speech... *(Other shouts of encouragement.)*

JOEY: Y'what? Me? Y'can frig that.

KEVIN: Yeah, go on, Joey... speech... speech...

JOEY: Well *I* ain't got nothin' to say. I think he's married the wrong bit...

KEVIN *and* NIDGE *simultaneously.*

KEVIN: ⎫ Joey, f'Christ's sake...
NIDGE: ⎭ Joey, can it, will yer —

JOEY *(finally persuaded):* All right... well... I'd just like to say... Alice is a very lucky girl... *(Shouts of 'Hear, Hear', 'Dead right' etc)*... an' if Kevin's still on the loose in two years time she'll be even luckier... *(Shrieks of laughter from* KEVIN'*s party.)*...hey c'mon now — Alice has landed herself a real prize there — *(More laughter.)*... I mean it — straight now. Our Alice says, give us the moon, Kevin... know what he'd do? I'll tell yer what — on with the gloves... straight up there... no fingerprints, no messing... *(More laughter.)*... assuming he could flog it over the odds when he got it down again... *(Laughter and applause.)* Okay, okay... I would like to propose a toast... I would like to raise a glass. *(He smashes an empty bottle and holds up the broken end.)* To Alice and Kevin... *(They all raise glasses.)* Kevin and Alice, may they rest in peace...

Toasts and cheers from KEVIN'*s side.* ALICE'*s side look faintly disgusted. Shouts from* KEVIN'*s table of 'Speech, speech'.* KEVIN *finally gets up.*

KEVIN: I'd just like to say… to all me mates an' that… ta for coming… an' for all the prezzies… wherever they come from… whatever much they didn't cost… an' to me newly-acquired sister-in-law, Janine, for bein' a smashin' bridesmaid…

JOEY: Even though she slapped his hands coming home in the car…

KEVIN: An' to Alice's mam an' dad — no doubt thinking, Christ, what's our Al got herself landed with?… look at it this way… yer not so much gaining a son as losing a daughter…

KEVIN *gets down amid cheers and shouts.* KEVIN *and* JOEY *settle down for some serious drinking at their table.* JANINE *has joined* NITA, BETH *and* PHIL *at their table.*

JANINE: Well, what are we now? February? I'll be an auntie by Christmas.

PHIL: A what?

JANINE: Well, y'know what it's like, Phil. Kev wants her at home…

PHIL: So?

JANINE: Well, she'll soon get bored ironing his socks. If she's gonna stop in, might as well keep fit fending off nappy rash.

PHIL: I don't believe this.

NIDGE *(coming over):* Hey Phil, how y'doing? Courting yet, are yer?

PHIL *(now beset on all sides):* Y'what?

NIDGE, *very drunk, tries to man-handle* PHIL.

NIDGE: Anyone special, hey? Nice lad? Do I know him?

PHIL: What sort of a word is 'courting'?

NITA: Are y'seeing anyone he means?

PHIL: I see lots of people.

NITA Phil…

PHIL: I see people who know what they're on about. Who got something worth listening to. Who think there's more to life than giving birth and getting buried.

PHIL *gets up and walks out.*

NIDGE: Seen that? Education for yer. University. Ignorant bitch.

KEVIN *(shouting across):* Hey Nidge, get us a taxi, will yer?

NIDGE: What, y'mean rob yer one…

NIDGE *goes out laughing to himself.* ALICE *and* KEVIN *are making a move to go.*

NITA *(eager to find an excuse to go):* Is it that late already…

ALICE *(seeing her preparing to leave):*
Oh, y'not leaving? They're all goin' into town.

NITA: Alice, I gotta get up. Getting the work done on me shop tomorrow.

BETH: Oh, me an' all. Got six hours solid kip to get in before tea time.

ALICE: Oh, are y'sure y'won't —

JOEY *(shouting over):* Hey, Alice — time to go — get yer clothes off.

ALICE *(trying to ignore him):* Listen… can I just say?… thanks for coming…

BETH *and* ALICE *kiss each other.*

BETH: I'll give yer a ring…

ALICE *kisses* NITA.

ALICE: I am dead happy, y'know.

NITA: Are you?

ALICE: It's what I wanted, Nita.

JOEY*(shouting):* Hey, Alice — get yer arse across here for the old man

ALICE: I'll have to go… *(She goes over to* KEVIN.*)*

JOEY *(springing across):* Sneaking off, are yer? Nobody fancy a quick poke behind the car park wall?

ALICE: Joey...

JOEY: Oh, hey, I forgot, didn't I? Y'got yer posh mates round. Did I show yer up, Alice? Did I disgust yer?

ALICE: You always disgust me, Joey.

NIDGE *(off, shouting):* Taxi's here.

ALICE: Are we…

JOEY: Is she startin' already?

KEVIN: C'mon you — let's get going… *(He puts his arm round* ALICE *and starts to take her out.)*

JOEY: Hey, where's yer manners, Kevin? *(He grabs* ALICE *violently and kisses her.)* Best man, aren't I?

KEVIN *sticks up a finger to* JOEY *and takes* ALICE *out.*

(To BETH *and* NITA:*)* Well, what can I do for you, girls? Any offers? Any requests?

BETH: Just one, Joey.

JOEY *(grabbing* JANINE*):* Looks like it's gonna be you, then.

JANINE *(as she is being led out):* I wouldn't bank on it. *(To* BETH *and* NITA:*)* I'll see yer, then.

JOEY: 'Night, girls.

JOEY *and* JANINE *go out.*

BETH: Y'walking?

NITA: Might as well. *(They are about to leave.)* Oh look…

BETH: What?

NITA: Look what she left behind…

She goes and picks up ALICE'S *wedding bouquet.* BETH *makes a face.* NITA *throws it at her.* BETH *dives out of the way.*

They go off together.

As the lights fade the sound of a train announcement can be heard saying: 'This is Bristol Temple Meads This is Bristol Temple Meads… British Rail apologise for the late arrival of the 19.55. from Manchester Piccadilly, due to arrive at 23.05…'

The lights come up on NASH, *at home, stretched out in a chair, reading.*

From offstage, the sound of a door closing and PHIL*'s voice saying 'Is he in?' Someone replies 'Yeah, his light's on.'*

NASH *turns in his chair so that he has his back to the door.* PHIL *comes in, carrying a hold-all, and stands in the doorway.* NASH *affects not to notice her. She stands unsure of what to do. Finally he turns round.*

PHIL: Well don't ask us in, Nash.

NASH *(going back to his book):* Yer back early.

PHIL: I didn't stay.

NASH: Never.

PHIL *(coming into the room):* Well what did *you* think?

NASH: Thought it might be good for yer.

PHIL: Well it wasn't. It was a shambles. I felt sick.

NASH: Y'shouldn't eat so much.

PHIL: Nash, it isn't funny.

NASH *(putting his book down):* Sick of what, Phil?

PHIL: Oh, I dunno. Everything. I hate it. I hate goin' back. The narrowness, the back-chat, the stupid jokes, the bitching in corners — 'Oh she must be queer, she got A Levels' — 'Oh, is that 'cos she can't get a feller?' — 'When y'gettin' married, Phil?' — 'What she needs is a good screw' — 'Or a good hiding'. Ha ha ha.

NASH: Ignore it.

PHIL: I can't. I hate it. All that 'salt-of-the-earth' solidarity makes me sick. Yer working-class, y'live in a dump — they think that's clever. Think it's a virtue in its own right. Well it's not. It doesn't excuse. It doesn't make it okay to be a narrow-minded, intolerant, foul-mouthed dickhead.

NASH: Like you, y'mean?

PHIL: Y'could at least sympathise. Or is it too close to World's End?

NASH: Wallsend, Phil. Though the distinction is minimal.

PHIL: Nash… don't you ever go home an' think, Christ, there but for the grace of God?

NASH: Yeah, I do go home.

PHIL: And what d'y'think?

NASH: There but for the grace of God?

PHIL (*picking up her bag and heading for the door*): It's not funny.

NASH: Y'not staying?

PHIL: I'm goin' back to Hall.

NASH: Well I'm not walkin' yer.

PHIL: So?

NASH: So y'might as well stay. PHIL *looks at him for a moment. His face gives nothing away. Finally she puts her bag down.*
The lights go down.

The lights come up on NITA's *salon.* ALICE *rushes on excitedly.* BETH *saunters on behind her and looks round, coolly appraising.*

BETH: Bit much, innit?

ALICE: God, Beth, wish I had a dad like that.

BETH: Not bad, is it? Come over here, can't write six words of English. Scrawl the odd prescription an' here he is settin' up shop for her.

ALICE (*picking up one of* NITA's *cards*):
'Nita Sharman welcomes you to Nita's Headlines Hairdressing Salon. Tinted mirrors… streamlined back-wash…'

BETH: Wall-to-wall fitted ferns.

ALICE: God, Beth, it's brill, though.

BETH (*acting it out*): 'Oh, come this way, madam … what can we do for you? You may be a dog … you may have a face like a bag of bruised plums, but we can transform you. Sheena Easton? Kate Bush? For the price of a cut, blow an' decent tip, even you can be Pamela Ewing. Now, how d'you like your music, madam? Loud? Deafening? Or sonic? What, goin' already? Not before a restyle, manicure, pedicure, sunbed, face lift? Oh, an' there's your bill, madam. That'll give you something to read on the way home.'

ALICE: S'all right for some.

BETH: Makes yer sick, dun't it? *She saunters off out.* ALICE *continues to gaze wistfully around her.* NITA *comes on and announces her presence with a fanfare.*

NITA: Well? What d'y'reckon?

Nita's salon, Lamda, 1988.

ALICE: Is it yours? Is it really all yours?

NITA: Mine an' no one else's!

ALICE: God, Nita, yer dead lucky, you are, having all this.

NITA: What d'y'mean 'lucky'? It's not a birthday present, y'know. It's my neck on the line.

ALICE: Oh yeah, but at least yer dad…

NITA: What d'y'mean me dad?

ALICE: Settin' yer up.

NITA: Oh, here we go again. 'It's all right for Nita. Her dad's a doctor, he's rakin' it in. Oh well, they all are, aren't they — these pakis.'

ALICE: Oh, hang on, Nita — I never said that.

NITA: Well forget about me dad. Me an' the bank manager, this is. No one else.

ALICE *(sudden thought):* Oh God... but s'pose nobody comes in…s'posing you have to close… s'posing it doesn't work…?

NITA: It will.

The phone rings. NITA *answers it.*

NITA *(as the lights go down):* Hello…Nita's Headlines

The lights come up again on the salon. NITA *is on the phone.*

NITA: Thank you… that'll be ten o'clock Wednesday for a cut and blow…

BETH *marches on, salutes and stands to attention.*

BETH: I did it.

NITA *(putting the phone down):* Did what?

BETH: Volunteered (NITA *looks blank.)* The army.

NITA *(as if she's heard it all before):* Really.

BETH *(performing it):* Information? Yeah, I come for information. I come on a recce. Committed? What's it look like? I'm here, aren't I? Know what I done last week? — I'll show yer 'committed' — y'know what? Seen *The Wild Geese* six times. Oh yeah, well there in't much I don't know about blowing people's balls off.

Question Number Two: Physical — right? Well cop this f'r'a specimen.

(She assumes a muscle-man pose.)

Rock hard, this is. *(Tapping her stomach.)* Solid rock.

I done two press-ups last week. Well not on the same day, obviously. Oh yeah, but ask us about marksmanship. Go on. Marksmanship? Now yer talking. I bin having a crack at me dad's air rifle … an' I'm getting pretty nifty. Oh yeah. Brought down — yesterday this is — brought down two japonicas an' an hanging basket. With one eye shut.

Yeah, right, okay — in traditional fields of armed warfare, what is the call — I know what yer saying — for gunning down a fuchsia? Okay, okay, fair question. Let me finish. It's not the fuchsias, is it? It's the principle.

Have y'seen *The Wild Geese*? Y'should, honest. It's invaluable. The tactics… the manoevres… the right attitude… the right face. Like…what's this? *(She assumes a horrible face. Then as if it's obvious.)* Roger Moore. *(She does another face, accompanied by a growl)* Richard Burton. Yeah. You have seen it, haven't yer?

Oh no, I'm not daft — I do know —

The Wild Geese is mercenaries, right? — which is not strictly the same as army. Yeah, but it's all the same in the long run, in't it? Join the army, learn to be a bastard — then go out there an' put all that skill into practice. Get a few wars goin'… stage the odd coup. Y'could retire on yer winnings by the time yer forty. Also… and this is a point worth thinking about… mercenaries don't pay income tax. Well… yeah… that is usually 'cos they're dead… but what a way to go, eh?

NITA: Beth… I don't know if you'd really be suited for the army.

BETH: What d'y'mean?

NITA: Bigoted… bad-tempered… loud-mouthed… aggressive… d'you want me to go on?

BETH: Yeah, right, I know. I'm overqualified. So I'll just have to go in as a general.

ALICE *and* KEVIN'S *house.*

ALICE *and* KEVIN *are sitting watching TV.* KEVIN *sits in a chair with* ALICE *at his feet. He is watching the TV intently but absent-mindedly stroking* ALICE's *hair as he does.*

KEVIN *(suddenly):* Aw watch this now — just watch — that's brilliant, that is.

ALICE: Could we have four?

KEVIN: Have what yer like.

ALICE *(slight pause):* When could I start? *(No reply.)* No, 'cos, what I mean is… once I know we're goin f'r'it…

KEVIN *(still glued to the TV)*: Sssssssssssshhhhhh…

ALICE: I could put me mind to it. I could start trying harder.

KEVIN: Well get yer skates on then.

ALICE *(delighted)*: Can I?

KEVIN: What y'askin' us for? Y'don't think about it, do yer? Y'just get on with it.

ALICE: Oh no, but y'should think about it, Kevin. Y'should.

KEVIN: Oh, where d'y'read that crap, Al? Having kids is easy. It's a piece of piss. *(Suddenly transfixed by the TV.)* Oh, look at that, Al — that's bloody great acting, that is.

ALICE: What is?

KEVIN: Bloke there with the pint in his hand. *(Seeing she's unconvinced.)* Yer bloody ignorant, you are, Al. I'm talking about genius.

ALICE *(snuggling up to him)*: Kevin…

KEVIN: Alice, d'y'mind? The adverts is on.

ALICE: I love you, Kevin.

KEVIN: Shut up, Al.

ALICE: I do.

KEVIN: Yeah, all right.

ALICE: D'you love me?

KEVIN: I married yer, didn't I?

ALICE: Oh… just say it, Kevin…

KEVIN: You're all right. *(He pushes her away, then absentmindedly strokes her hair, still intent on the TV. Suddenly, the sound of the door. JOEY comes in.)*

JOEY: All right newly weds? All right Kevin? *(To ALICE:)* What you doin' layin' on yer backside. Y'got no ironing to do? Hey, y'wanna watch that Kev, y'know — two weeks time, she'll have yer making yer own dinner.

KEVIN *(to ALICE)*: Go on, then — up you get.

ALICE: What d'y'mean?

KEVIN: Let's have some tea on. (JOEY *smiles in encouragement.*)

ALICE *(getting up, annoyed)*: Is he stopping?

JOEY: In't yer pleased to see me, Al?

KEVIN *(reproachfully)*: Alice…

(ALICE *stalks off into the kitchen.*)

JOEY: Well?

KEVIN: No.

JOEY: No what?

KEVIN: I in't told her.

JOEY: What y'bin doin' Kev? Y've had a week.

KEVIN: Oh, what can I say, Joey? You wanna try tellin' her?

JOEY: Hey, *I'll* tell her — y'want me to tell her? Hey, Alice.

KEVIN: No. Don't. I'll do it.

JOEY: All right then. We moving this week?

KEVIN: Cross Lane Warehouse?

JOEY: I'm skint, Kevin. An' Carly's got a stack of orders this high for Sonys.

KEVIN: Yeah, I'm easy. Thursday?

JOEY: Tomorrow.

KEVIN: Nah, s'no good, I'm out.

JOEY: Where?

KEVIN: Round her mam's.

JOEY: Yer joking, aren't yer? Eight, nine hundred, two-way split — Are we in this game, or aren't we, Kevin?

KEVIN: I said I'd go, Joey. Okay? An' if we're gonna keep this hush, I can't go breaking arrangements two weeks into me marriage. I'll do Thursday.

JOEY: Oh yeah — we get there, find half of Salford's beat us to it? (KEVIN *refuses to argue.*) I know what, Kev — I think yer goin' soft.

KEVIN: I didn't get married for a joke, y'know.

JOEY: Oh, what, Kev? — Y'love her, do yer?

KEVIN *(sheepishly):* Yeah, I do as a matter of fact.

JOEY *(sentimental):* Aaaah, Kevin

KEVIN: What?

JOEY: You soft bastard.

Nita, Alice, Danny, Beth and Phil at the finals of the hairdressing competition, Lamda, 1988.

Extract B

Act 2

The Ritz Ballroom in Manchester.

The night of the competition. BETH *is sitting at a table laden with drinks.* ALICE *is pacing up and down being comforted by* PHIL. *In the background, music and the sound of people talking and drinking.*

ALICE: Where is she?

PHIL: She'll be here.

ALICE: What is she doing? *(Refusing to be calmed.)* She's gonna miss it — she is — I could kill her.

PHIL: Alice, calm down... *Enter* CARMEN *(with a ridiculously flamboyant hairstyle) accompanied by* REUBEN.

CARMEN *(as she comes in):* Course, I coulda been a model — I was asked — I got perfect hair — but y'don't like to draw attention t'yerself, do yer?

REUBEN: Evening all... Danny Boy not in yet?

BETH: He's on his way.

REUBEN: C'mon, park yerself, Carmen — yer making the place look untidy. (CARMEN *sits down.*) Right, I'll get them in ... *(He goes off to get some drinks.)*

ALICE *(still pacing about)*: I'll be sick. I will. I'll blow it all wrong. I'll be disqualified... oh God, where is she, Phil?...

PHIL: Alice, just sit down...

Suddenly NITA *rushes in, looking as if she's about to collapse.*

ALICE *(springing up, almost screaming):* Where y'been? Y'nearly missed it.

CARMEN: We thought y'wasn't coming — y'nearly give us heart failure.

PHIL: Nita, are you all right?

NITA: I'm okay... I just feel a bit

PHIL: Nita, sit down — d'y'wanna drink? *(To* BETH:) Can y'get her a drink?

NITA: No, I don't want a drink.

ALICE: Is it nerves?

CARMEN: Oh, it's nerves.

NITA *(snapping):* It's not nerves.

REUBEN *(coming in with drinks):* Here y'are then... oh, don't tell me — pissed before it's even started.

BETH: Have y'took anything?

NITA: I don't want anything.

CARMEN: Y'should — oh, y'should, Nita...

NITA: Where's Danny? He's s'posed to be here.

ALICE: He's coming.

REUBEN: Tied up in the shop, is he? *(Nudging* CARMEN.)

BETH: C'mon Nita, have this... *(She gives her some water.)*

Over the loudspeaker comes the announcement 'Will all competitors please report to their places?'

ALICE: Nita, it's starting...

BETH: C'mon, Nita, get yer skates on. NITA *tries to compose herself*

NITA *(getting up):* I'm all right… *(Then nearly collapses.)* I can't… I can't stand up…
Phil, I'm gonna pass out… *(She sits with her head between her knees, shaking.)*
DANNY *runs on, at first not realizing what's happening.*
DANNY: Nita, I'm sorry — I couldn't park… Nita?
PHIL: She's not well.
DANNY: Nita, y'all right, babe?
CARMEN: I don't think she should go on. (BETH *glares at her.)* That's what I think,
anyway.
DANNY: What's the matter with her?
CARMEN: Nerves.
ALICE *(snapping):* It's not nerves.
CARMEN: Well I think she'd be better off in bed.
REUBEN: Too right.
ALICE: Phil, what we gonna do?
REUBEN: Hey Danny — should have a word with the judges. How much cash y'got on yer?
CARMEN: Best get her home. I would. D'y'want some valium?
PHIL: No.
DANNY: What?
PHIL: She's not goin' home.
DANNY: Oh, I dunno, Phil…
PHIL: She's not copping out that easy —
DANNY: Look at the state of her, Phil.
PHIL: I seen the state on her, Danny.
DANNY *(getting annoyed):* You taking charge now, Phil?
BETH *(eagerly stepping in):* Tell him, Phil.
DANNY *(turning on her):* You keep yer nose out, you.
BETH: Up yours, Danny.
PHIL *(ignoring them all)*: Get up, Nita.
DANNY: Leave her, Phil.
PHIL: Get up, Nita.
NIITA: I can't, Phil —
PHIL: You can — get up — stop acting soft —
ALICE *(looking worried):* We'll have to go — they're ready to start
PHIL *picks up a glass of water from the table.*
PHIL: Nita… *(Louder:)* Nita

NITA *looks up.* PHIL *throws the water in her face. There is a rush to protect* NITA *and
fend* PHIL *off, but* PHIL *pushes them away.*
Get off her — leave her alone… *(Very softly.)* Nita, c'mon, get up…
NITA: I can't, Phil —
PHIL: Yes… you can, Nita… *(Suddenly losing her temper, dragging her up.)* Get up, Nita…
DANNY: What d'y'think yer doing, Phil.
PHIL: Gettin' me own back.
DANNY: What for?
PHIL: That earache I copped two years ago.
NITA: What earache?

PHIL: Don't come that with me. Two years ago — go on, Phil, get out, Phil — go to college, do something. Rings a bell, Nita? I was looking for quiet life an' all.

NITA: I'm not looking for a quiet life.

PHIL: Y'not gonna get one. *(She pulls her up.)* I didn't.

Now with NITA *on her feet,* PHIL *is roughly cleaning up her face.*

An' this is my way of saying thank you.

Grabbing her arm.

Get upon that stage, Nita… get hold of her, Alice… (ALICE *hesitates.)* — do as I say, Alice… grab her arm… right, now move…

One on either side, they both drag NITA *off.*

DANNY, CARMEN *and* REUBEN *are amazed.*

In the background the loudspeaker is heard 'Ladies and Gentlemen, the Manchester heat of this year's Colour Trophy Competition is now about to begin.

BETH: Right then — we gettin' a few bevvies in while it gets going?

A corridor outside the main room.

PHIL *is walking up and down trying to keep calm.* DANNY, *with* REUBEN *in attendance, is pacing about the opposite side of the corridor.*

PHIL: I wish I smoked. I might have some nails left.

DANNY *(pacing up and down)*: Christ, I feel like she's givin' birth out there.

REUBEN: Oh, that's a good one, hey Danny? *(Laughing to himself)*

DANNY *(coming over to* PHIL*)*: She's blown it. She has, Phil. She won't even get placed.

PHIL: An' where would she be if *you'd* had yer own way?

DANNY: Me?

PHIL: Dosed to the eyeballs in bed, feeling sorry for herself? Perfect cop out.

DANNY: Phil, you saw the state on her. She was ill.

PHIL: She was not ill. *(Pause.)* She was terrified.

DANNY: What of?

PHIL: Not winning.

REUBEN: Christ, he could really do with being halfway up the M1 when the scores get read out.

PHIL: Fat lot of use he'll be there.

REUBEN: *She's* terrified? He's fuckin' petrified. You tried bein' around when she's not getting her own way?

PHIL: Two years I've not been around — precisely *because* she got her own way.

DANNY: I shoulda took her home. *(No one replies.)* Oh Christ, what'm I gonna say to her? If she dun't get placed, I'd rather she had an excuse.

There is a moment of sympathy between them, broken by REUBEN.

REUBEN: Oh yeah, an' Stockport County might win the Cup next season.

PHIL: Danny, she shouldn't *have* an excuse.

REUBEN *(to* PHIL*)*: You, y'love arguments, don't yer?

PHIL *(to* DANNY*)*: Well, she'll just have to learn to be a gracious loser, won't she?

Back inside the main ballroom. Round the table CARMEN *is lounging about trying to look glamorous while* BETH *is waiting for* PHIL *to come back.* REUBEN *and* DANNY *come in, followed by* PHIL. *The* COMPERE *can be heard announcing the finalists. His commentary runs under and simultaneously with the dialogue between* DANNY, BETH, PHIL, REUBEN, CARMEN, NITA *and* ALICE.

BETH Christ, he loves the sound of his own voice, doesn't he?

DANNY *(irritated):* Beth...

BETH: I'm not out with you now.

BETH *joins in the screams.*

Bobby Charlton? What does *he* know about hair?

PHIL (suddenly) What's she doin'. She's meant to stop onstage.

REUBEN: Blown it. Definitely.

CARMEN: Oh God, she looks terrible.

NITA *comes in as if from the stage.* ALICE, *looking anxious, has followed her.*

NITA: I blew it.

DANNY: Nita, you all right, babe?

NITA: I really cocked it up.

BETH: Looks all right from here.

NITA: It's not. It's a shambles.

DANNY: It doesn't matter, Nita.

NITA: It matters to me.

CARMEN: Next year, Nita...

NITA: I don't want it next year. I want it now.

ALICE: Nita, *I* saw what you did. It was good. It was really good.

NITA: No, it wasn't, Alice.

ALICE: It was. There was no difference.

NITA: I was pathetic. I had about as much skill as a carthorse.

DANNY: Nita, c'mere... *(He puts his arm round her.)* You'll get it next year.

REUBEN: If we have to bribe all the judges and ship the rest of the competition to Siberia.

NITA *(suddenly):* I'll have a drink.

ALICE: You sure?

NITA *(picking up a drink):* To next year.

DANNY *(glad of the diversion)* To next year...

BETH: How d'you get on, Alice?

ALICE: Oh, okay, y'know — I was pleased with it.

NITA *(suddenly remembering* ALICE*):* You looked great, Alice. Y'looked really good.

ALICE I think it's the best I've done — I mean, for *me* it was the best — *(Raising her glass.)* This is to next year, Nita...

They half-catch the mention of ALICE'S *name.*

NITA: What? —

ALICE: *Me?*

COMPERE *(off):* Ladies and gentlemen, the judges have now made up their minds... and I know you'll agree that the standard this year has been exceptionally high — I think I can say our highest ever — and that definitely goes for the turn-out — an amazing two hundred and sixteen entries, all vying for those top ten places and the Grand Final in London... well, I certainly don't envy the judge their work tonight, do you?

COMPERE *(off):* And I'd just like you to give a big hand to all the judges... and to our special guests... Simon Le Bon... *(Sounds of screams in the background.)* And world-famous football personality... Bobby Charlton!

COMPERE *(off):* So... before we go on to the results, I'd just like to tell you what's in store for this year's winner... *(He continues in the background.)* Well of course all the top ten finalists receive a diploma and a sash... that goes for the boys too! ... The winner of the Grand Final will receive a cheque for two hundred and fifty pounds... yes that's *two hundred and fifty pounds*... a magnificent silver trophy and... the opportunity to represent England as part of the World Cup team who will be travelling to Mexico for the World Hairdressing Finals next year!... And as you look around you, ladies and gentlemen, at this truly inspirational display of hairdressing expertise you see before you... just remember, this is where you saw them first — the styles, the fashions... whether you like it or not ... *these* are the styles you will be wearing *next year*! ... Yes, that's right... *truly inspirational.* And meanwhile... what about a big hand for all those *truly marvellous* girls — *and* boys... mustn't forget those boys, must we?... — all those boys and girls who have taken part in this year's competition... *as models...*

There is a sound of applause. The COMPERE *continues in the background ad lib, until:*

Ladies and gentlemen... I've just been handed a slip of paper... that magic piece of paper... which contains the names of this year's top ten winners...

Sounds of applause.

So without further ado... here... in ascending order... are the results of the Manchester heat of the 1981 Colour Trophy...

In tenth position... Are you all ready out there?...

In tenth position... Ladies and gentlemen... From Stockport... Table Number 62... Philip Yates...

Sounds of applause.

In ninth position... and remember... all the top ten go to the Grand Final in London... from Salford... Table Number 75. Alice Gilmore...

Sounds of applause.

BETH: *You?* —

PHIL: Al, it's you — it is!

ALICE *(in hysterics):* It's me! It's me!

BETH *(grabbing hold of her):* Go on, go on… it's you… get up there

ALICE *rushes off amid general applause.*

BETH *(dancing about):* Nice one, Al!

NITA: She deserved that… she worked dead hard. I'm dead pleased for her… *(She bursts into tears.)*

DANNY *(out of his depth):* Nita?… come on, Nita… *(putting his arm round her.)*

NITA: I'm dead proud of her.

PHIL: She did well, Nita. Next year *you'll* do it.

BETH *(doing a football salute):* Yeah, dead right! No messing.

NITA: I think I'm gonna go.

BETH: Nah, y'can't go.

DANNY *(at a loss):* D'you want me to come with you?

NITA: No, it's okay… I'm all right… She is about to go.

BETH: Nita, I'm not kidding, if that thing up there with red an' black stripes wins, I'm gonna lynch that Simon Le Bon.

NITA *(to PHIL):* Tell Alice I'm dead pleased for her…

She goes out.

BETH *watches her go.*

BETH *(to DANNY):* Go with yer, y'dick.

DANNY: I can't. What can I say?

BETH: Danny, yer a wanker, you are.

DANNY *(getting annoyed):* Hey, you'll be out if you don't watch it.

BETH: Y'what? Me job? Working f'r'a wanker like *you?* You know where y'can stuff it, Danny…

DANNY: Yer askin' for something, you are… *(He is about to grab BETH.)*

Everyone is momentarily stunned, then suddenly it sinks in.

BETH: Nita! —

PHIL: She did it! —

BETH: The daft get — where is she? *(Shouting to make herself heard above the cheers.)* Nita, where are yer?* NITA *suddenly appears in the doorway.*

In eighth position… from Cheadle Hulme… Table Number 116… Joseph Heywood

Applause.

In seventh position… from Stretford… Table Number 52… Helen Foxdecker…

Applause.

In sixth position… from Irlam… Table Number 178… Michael Dobson…

Applause.

In fifth place… from Eccles… Table Number 202… Gina Dinsdale Fewkes

Applause.

In fourth place… from Whalley Range… Table Number 98… Flora Mackintosh…

Applause.

In 3rd place… ladies and gentlemen from Old Trafford… Table Number 7… Ronnie Atkinson…

Applause.

And the runner-up in this year's heat from Altrincham… Table Number 17… Marcus Wright…

Applause.

And in First Place… the winner of the 1981 Manchester heat… Ladies and gentlemen From Salford… Table Number 74… Nita Sharman!

Prolonged applause.

NITA *(almost a whisper):* I won it. *(Screams.)* I won it!

Everyone rushes to congratulate her.

PHIL *(rushing her forward)*: Nita, get up there and take it.

NITA *goes off onto the stage. The applause is now deafening.* CARMEN *prepares to take photographs.* REUBEN *rushes on with champagne.*

NITA *and* ALICE *come back with their sashes and awards. Photos are taken, streamers thrown. Everyone joins in the congratulations.*

PHIL *is standing apart from the rest, watching.* NITA *sees her, goes up to her and puts the trophy into her hand.*

NITA: One-all, Phil.

Suddenly the sound stops dead. The lights are out except on PHIL *who now comes forward.*

PHIL: One-all? Is it? Did you just equalise, Nita?

Look at yer now. Name on the sheet.

Alice an' all. That's a turn-up for the book.

Me an' Beth — we're a joke. What've we been doing? Twin strikers, never got past the halfway line. While you two stuffy gets come sneaking up the wing an' lob one in from forty yards. Man of the Match. Both of yer. Now what? Change tack? Swap sides? Beth just pulled her shirt on by the looks of it. No more sitting with the subs for Beth. Watch yer backs out there — she'll break yer neck. And me? Oh, the boss is saying, too speculative, too much time-wasting. Get yer sleeves rolled up, Phil. Y'got another half to play — y'could score a hat-trick. This lot's shown yer how it's done. So get out there... and break the net!

Blackout

Understanding action and structure

The play begins in Extract A with the marriage of Alice and Kevin, watched and commented on by Alice's friends. We are then swiftly led into the reception where characters and action provide the sense of a working-class 'do' that is fuelled by serious drinking and passing flirtation. The narrative (or story) then takes us into Phil's student existence in Bristol, Nita's new ladies' hairdressing business and Alice's family life.

- Why does Phil say, 'I don't like funerals' and where does this idea crop up again in the extract?

- What do you think Phil's view of Kevin is, and what evidence do you have?

- What kind of married life do Kevin and Alice have and what is the main threat to it?

Extract B is the conclusion of the play and is a scene of mounting expectation and excitement. Both Nita and Alice (who now works with Nita, following the break up of her marriage) have entered a local hairdressing competition. However Nita's preparations have been seriously disrupted by the violent intervention of Joey, extracting money with threats and spoiling Nita's newly fledged successes.

- How does this ending compare to the opening scenes in Extract A?
- Why does Phil speak so harshly to Nita in the lines beginning 'Get up Nita…' on page 62?
- What is the overall feeling of the last scene?

Understanding character

The main characters in the *Red Devils Trilogy* are:

Alice

Beth

Nita

Phil.

In the first play of the trilogy, their identities were established and in *True Dare Kiss* they are developed further. Horsfield also introduces us to other characters, especially male ones, which enables the drama to explore sexual relationships.

In her notes to the Methuen's text of the trilogy Horsfield warns us of a possible difficulty with one character when she writes: 'Of the four central characters it is Phil's which tends to create the most problems … unless it is taken as a fundamental premise that of the four girls she is the most naturally affectionate, the most passionate, has the strongest sense of humour and always acts with the best (if sometimes mistaken) intentions.'

She also goes on to write that it is 'emphatically not my desire' to create male characters who should be viewed unsympathetically, as if she had a 'strong feminist axe to grind'. This is obviously an important point for her to make about her plays and we need to see how effective her attempts at characterisation of males has been.

- What do the following lines in Extract A tell us of the character of Alice, as she talks to Nita?

> See Phil's not speaking to me *(they both look at Phil)*. You tell her, Nita, bein' married's great. Y'get new clothes, y'get your yer picture took — and all them prezzies… see all that? That's my home, that is perched up there, top of the piano. Tell Phil she dun't know what she's been missing.
> (NITA *is on the verge of tears and pretends to have something in her eye to hide it)*
> Hey, did I show yer me ring? It's not the one I asked for but Kevin says it's got more class. I don't know where he got the money…

- What do you make of the character of Joey as he appears in Extract A?
- What are your reactions to Phil's character as shown by her words and actions in both extracts?

Understanding themes

Opportunity

The central theme of *True Dare Kiss* is opportunity, how that can open up or close and how it affects the lives of working-class girls (they are all 19 at the start of the play) as they move into adult life. We see Alice entering marriage, Phil at university, Beth thrashing around for meaning in her life and Nita taking on a business. These central threads all draw together as the play develops and a clear meaning comes through: opportunity is there, you must make your own life and future, because no-one else will do that for you.

Sexual relationships

Obviously the other main theme is sexual relationships and each of the four main characters has a very different approach to men.

- What comes across in the conversation between Phil and Nash in Extract A?
- How is Nita's business venture treated in the scene between Nita, Alice and Beth?
- Look closely at the following:

> BETH *(acting it out):* 'Oh come this way, madam… You may be a dog… you may have a face like a bag of bruised plums, but we can transform you. Sheena Easton? Kate Bush? For the price of a cut, blow an' decent tip, even you can be Pamela Ewing…'

- What does Extract B tell us about opportunity?

Understanding dramatic devices

Language

Horsfield's language in the *Red Devils Trilogy* is very realistic and at times she is forced to use strong colloquialisms in order to make her speech believable. Her dialogue reflects the speech of young people on the streets in Manchester in the early 1980s.

The language of the play changes to suit the dramatic purpose, so you need to look at the way in which language is used for effect in Extract B.

- Look at Phil's opening speech in Extract A. What examples can you find of slang and informal language here?
- Do you think the language is realistic? How does it differ from the language of other plays you have seen or read?

Conflict

There is a very good use of conflict in the latter part of Extract A where Joey interrupts Alice and Kevin at home. This enables the drama to deepen and it provides a problem that will be a key part of the play as it develops. As an audience we find ourselves drawn into the conflict between characters and we take sides.

- Where do you think Horsfield wants our sympathies to lie in this episode?

Contrast

The scenes between Nash and Phil, and Alice and Kevin serve as a contrast. We are meant to look at one couple and compare them to the other couple. This device allows Horsfield to examine the relationships of the two couples.

- What are the main differences between the Nash/Phil scene and the Kevin/Alice scenes?

Understanding performance

Pace

The *Red Devils Trilogy* moves very quickly and there is a very vivid sense of dramatic pace. Look at the way in which Alice's relationship with Kevin is established in Extract A. These brief scenes are meant to cover a period of several months in their married life.

- What aspects of their life together are not examined?

On the other hand, Extract B is meant to take place over the space of a few hours and so the sense of pace and time is different.

Setting and staging

Debbie Horsfield writes in her notes to the trilogy: 'The trilogy was originally written for a small studio space, with a low budget which allowed for minimal settings and costume changes… As a general comment on the staging of these plays, the more complicated and fussy the design, the less fluent and engaging the narrative.'

Horsfield suggests that scene changes can be suggested with lighting changes and little more.

- How effective is the change from one scene to another and how do you think these would work in performance?
- What is the importance of off-stage sounds and noises to the staging of each scene? For instance, you might want to look at the opening of Extract A.
- How would the acting of the opening of Extract B help an audience to understand what is going on?

Tasks

Personal response: writing

1   Write a short scene between two characters where one character advises the other not to do something (for instance, not get married, or not get involved with someone, or not mix with a certain group of people).

2   Joey is clearly a threat to the marriage of Alice and Kevin. What actions do you think Alice should take at the end of Extract A?

3   Write a newspaper article entitled: 'Opportunities for Young People in a New Century'.

4   This picture of working-class life is not always very flattering or complimentary. Horsfield tries to present to an audience the difficulties that affect the lives of ordinary people.

What are your feelings as you read the extracts?

You should write about:

a) the characters

b) the events

c) the main themes.

Practical activities

Individually or in pairs

5   Write a letter from Phil to Alice after she has heard of Alice's plans to marry Kevin.

6   Prepare a short speech for a wedding of one of your friends, or a person you know. Include in your speech:

a) what you know of your friend's character

b) stories about your friend, funny or otherwise

c) hopes for the future.

In groups

7   Look at the character of Joey as he appears in Extract A and create a continuation scene for him, using some characters from the play, and creating some new ones. Now act out your scene.

8   Allocate parts for Extract B and act it out so that the sense of occasion is brought out by paying attention to:

a) the announcer's speech

b) conversation

c) the emotions of the characters.

Useful notes

Please note that the dialogue in *True Dare Kiss* is extremely informal and it would not make sense to comment on all examples.

Extract A

wanna, coulda	examples of the use of Manchester dialect
Stretford End	part of Old Trafford football ground
Bristol Temple Meads	to indicate a change of location, a staging device
Hall	student hall of residence
Sheena Easton, Kate Bush	late 1970s, early 1980s pop singers, with distinctive hair styles
Pamela Ewing	character from Dallas an American soap opera
Salford	near Manchester

Extract B

get yer skates on	hurry up
valium	a tranquilliser, a prescription drug
Simon Le Bon	pop singer, member of pop group Duran Duran, popular in the 1980s
Bobby Charlton	former Manchester United footballer

Women Writers: Shelagh Delaney and Charlotte Keatley

Background and context

Shelagh Delaney, who was born in Salford in 1939, adapted *A Taste of Honey* from a novel that she had written as a teenager. The play was read by a very influential figure in the theatre at the time, Joan Littlewood of the Theatre Workshop. She gave Delaney important advice and enabled the play to be produced.

A Taste of Honey was first produced in 1958 to tremendous critical acclaim. The famous critic Kenneth Tynan, writing in *The Observer* said that 'Miss Delaney brings real people on to her stage… she is busy recording the wonder of life as she lives it'. The play went on to become a very successful film starring Rita Tushingham, and Shelagh Delaney continued to write plays and film scripts.

Charlotte Keatley was born in London in 1960 but moved to Manchester to study. Like Delaney, she was only young when she wrote *My Mother Said I Never Should*, a play which covers the relationships between four generations of women in one family. The play, initially rejected in a playwriting competition, was first performed in 1987 at the Contact Theatre, Manchester. It then went on to great success in London and has been performed throughout Europe and the world.

Both these plays have at their heart a serious social issue of the age: young single mothers and the difficulties they face in coping with pregnancy and motherhood. *A Taste of Honey* was seen as groundbreaking when it was first produced because the issue was generally ignored. *My Mother Said I Never Should* is written for a more sympathetic age although the problems that Jackie has to face are still very real. Both plays also deal with the relationships between mothers and daughters, although Delaney's family is very working class while Keatley writes about a more middle-class family.

A Taste of Honey

Act 2, Scene 1

[*Music. Enter* HELEN.]

HELEN: Jo! Your beloved old lady's arrived. Well, where is she, Romeo?

GEOF: Don't tell her I came for you.

HELEN: What? Don't mumble.

GEOF: I said don't tell her I came for you.

HELEN: All right, all right. This place hasn't changed much, has it? Still the same old miserable hole. Well, where's the lady in question?

GEOF: In there.

HELEN: What, lazing in bed, as usual? Come on, get up; plenty of girls in your condition have to go out to work and take care of a family. Come on, get up.

JO: What blew you in?

HELEN: Let's have a look at you.

JO: Who told you about me?

HELEN: Nobody.

JO: How did you get to know then?

HELEN: Come on, aren't you going to introduce me to your boy friend? Who is he?

JO: My boy friend. Oh, it's all right, we're so decent we're almost dead. I said who told you about me?

HELEN: Does it matter?

JO: I told you to keep out of my affairs, Geoffrey. I'm not having anybody running my life for me. What do you think you're running? A 'Back to Mother' movement?

GEOF: Your mother has a right to know.

JO: She's got no rights where I'm concerned.

HELEN: Oh, leave him alone. You're living off him, by all accounts.

JO: Who've you been talking to? That old hag downstairs?

Jo (Frances Cuka) centre stage in a production directed by Joan Littlewood at the Theatre Royal, Stratford, 1959.

HELEN: I didn't need to talk to her. The whole district knows what's been going on here.

JO: And what has been going on?

HELEN: I suppose you think you can hide yourself away in this chicken run, don't you? Well, you can't. Everybody knows.

GEOF: She won't go out anywhere, not even for a walk and a bit of fresh air. That's why I came to you.

HELEN: And what do you think I can do about it? In any case, bearing a child doesn't place one under an obligation to it.

GEOF: I should have thought it did.

HELEN: Well, you've got another think coming. If she won't take care of herself that's her lookout. And don't stand there looking as if it's my fault.

GEOF: It's your grandchild.

HELEN: Oh, shut up, you put years on me. Anyway, I'm having nothing to do with it. She's more than I can cope with, always has been.

GEOF: That's obvious.

HELEN: And what's your part in this little Victorian melodrama? Nursemaid?

JO: Serves you right for bringing her here, Geof.

HELEN: It's a funny-looking set-up to me.

JO: It's our business.

HELEN: Then don't bring me into it. Where's the loving father? Distinguished by his absence, I suppose.

JO: That's right.

HELEN [*to* GEOF]: Did she hear any more of him?

JO: No, she didn't.

HELEN: When I'm talking to the organ grinder I don't expect the monkey to answer.

JO: I could get him back tomorrow if I wanted to.

HELEN: Well, that's nice to know. He certainly left you a nice Christmas box. It did happen at Christmas, I suppose? When the cat's away.

GEOF: You've been away a long time.

HELEN: Oh, you shut up. Sling your hook!

JO: Will you keep out of this, Geoffrey?

HELEN: Well, come on, let's have a look at you. [JO *turns away.*] What's up? We're all made the same, aren't we?

JO: Yes we are.

HELEN: Well then. Can you cut the bread on it yet? [JO *turns.*] Yes, you're carrying it a bit high, aren't you? Are you going to the clinic regularly? Is she working?

GEOF: No, I told you, she doesn't like people looking at her.

HELEN: Do you think people have got nothing better to do than look at you?

JO: Leave me alone.

HELEN: She'd be better off working than living off you like a little bloodsucker.

GEOF: She doesn't live off me.

JO: No, we share everything, see! We're communists too.

HELEN: That's his influence I suppose.

JO: Get out of here. I won't go out if I don't want to. It's nothing to do with you. Get back to your fancy man or your husband, or whatever you like to call him. [HELEN *begins to chase her.*] Aren't you afraid he'll run off and leave you if you let him out of your sight?

HELEN: I'll give you such a bloody good hiding in a minute, if you're not careful. That's what you've gone short of!

JO: Don't show yourself up for what you are!

HELEN: You couldn't wait, could you? Now look at the mess you've landed yourself in.

JO: I'll get out of it, without your help.

HELEN: You had to throw yourself at the first man you met, didn't you?

JO: Yes, I did, that's right.

HELEN: You're man mad.

JO: I'm like you.

HELEN: You know what they're calling you round here? A silly little whore!

JO: Well, they all know where I get it from too.

HELEN: Let me get hold of her! I'll knock her bloody head round!

JO: You should have been locked up years ago, with my father.

HELEN: Let me get hold of her!

GEOF: Please, Jo, Helen, Jo, please!

HELEN: I should have got rid of you before you were born.

JO: I wish you had done. You did with plenty of others, I know.

HELEN: I'll kill her. I'll knock the living daylights out of her.

GEOF: Helen, stop it, you will kill her!

JO: If you don't get out of here I'll … jump out of the window.

[There is a sudden lull.]

GEOF *[yelling]*: Will you stop shouting, you two?

HELEN: We enjoy it.

GEOF: Helen!

HELEN: Now you're going to listen to a few home truths, my girl.

JO: We've had enough home truths!

HELEN: All right, you thought you knew it all before, didn't you? But you came a cropper. Now it's 'poor little Josephine, the tragedy queen, hasn't life been hard on her'. Well, you fell down, you get up … nobody else is going to carry you about. Oh, I know you've got this pansified little freak to lean on, but what good will that do you?

JO: Leave Geof out of it!

HELEN: Have you got your breath back? Because there's some more I've got to get off my chest first.

JO: You don't half like the sound of your own voice.

GEOF: If I'd known you were going to bully her like this I'd never have asked you to come here.

HELEN: You can clear off! Take your simpering little face out of it!

JO: Yes, buzz off, Geof! Well, who brought her here? I told you what sort of a woman she was. Go and … go and make a cup of tea.

[He goes.]

HELEN: Look at your arms. They're like a couple of stalks! You look like a ghost warmed up. And who gave you that haircut, him? Don't sit there sulking.

JO: I thought it was the tea break.

HELEN: I didn't come here to quarrel.

JO: No?

HELEN: I brought you some money.

JO: You know what you can do with that.

HELEN: All right! You've said your piece. Money doesn't grow on trees. I'll leave it on the table. Have you been collecting your maternity benefit or …

JO: Or are you too idle to walk down to the post office? Don't be daft! I'm not entitled to it. I haven't been earning long enough.

HELEN: You've no need to go short of anything.

JO: It's taken you a long time to come round to this, hasn't it?

HELEN: What?

JO: The famous mother-love act.

HELEN: I haven't been able to sleep for thinking about you since he came round to our house.

JO: And your sleep mustn't be disturbed at any cost.

HELEN: There'll be money in the post for you every week from now on.

JO: Until you forget.

HELEN: I don't forget things; it's just that I can't remember anything. I'm going to see you through this whether you like it or not. After all I am …

JO: After all you are my mother! You're a bit late remembering that, aren't you? You walked through that door with that man and didn't give me a second thought.

HELEN: Why didn't you tell me?

JO: You should have known. You're nothing to me. [PETER *appears.*]

PETER: What the hell's going on? Do you expect me to wait in the filthy street all night?

HELEN: I told you to stay outside.

PETER: Don't point your bloody finger at me.

HELEN: I said I'd only be a few minutes and I've only been a few minutes. Now come on, outside!

PETER: Ah! The erring daughter. There she is. *[Sings.]* 'Little Josephine, you're a big girl now.' Where d'you keep the whisky?

HELEN: They haven't got any. Now, come on.

PETER *[seeing* GEOF]: What's this, the father? Oh Christ, no!

GEOF: Who's he?

HELEN: President of the local Temperance Society!

PETER *[singing]:* 'Who's got a bun in the oven? Who's got a cake in the stove?'

HELEN: Leave her alone.

PETER: Oh, go to hell!

JO: I've got nothing to say.

PETER: Go on, have your blasted family reunion, don't mind me! *[Notices* GEOF *again.]* Who's this? Oh, of course! Where are the drinks, Lana? *[He falls into the kitchen, singing.]* 'Getting to know you, getting to know all about you …'

HELEN: Jo, come on …

[There is a loud crash in the kitchen.]

And the light of the world shone upon him. [PETER *enters.*]

PETER: Cheer up, everybody. I am back. Who's the lily? Look at Helen, well, if she doesn't look like a bloody unrestored oil painting. What's the matter everybody? Look at the sour-faced old bitch! Well, are you coming for a few drinks or aren't you?

HELEN: The pubs aren't open yet.

JO: Do you mind getting out of here?

PETER: Shut your mouth, bubble belly! Before I shut it for you. Hey! *[To* GEOF.] Mary, come here. Did I ever tell you about the chappie who married his mother by mistake?

JO: I said get him out of here, Helen. His breath smells.

HELEN: I can't carry him out, can I?

PETER: His name was Oedipus, he was a Greek I think. Well, the old bag turned out to be his mother …

HELEN: Shut up, Peter, for God's sake!

PETER: So he scratched out both his eyes.

HELEN: Cut the dirty stories!

PETER: But I only scratched out one of mine. Well, are YOU coming or not?

HELEN: I'm not.

PETER: Well, is anybody coming for a few drinks? You staying with the ladies, Jezebel?

GEOF: Listen, mister, this is my friend's flat.

PETER: And what do you do, Cuddles? Don't worry, I know this district. Look at Helen, isn't she a game old bird? Worn out on the beat but she's still got a few good strokes left.

HELEN: Get out of here, you drunken sot.

Jo (Frances Cuka) and Helen (Avis Bunnage), at rehearsals for 'A Taste of Honey', 1959.

PETER: Now I told you to moderate your language. What's this? Giving my money away again?

HELEN: Take your bloody money and get out!

PETER: Thank you.

HELEN: You dirty bastard!

PETER: You should have heard her the other night. You know what happened? Her wandering boy returned. He hadn't been home for two weeks and do you know why? He picked up a couple of grapefruit on a thirty-two bust, rich, young and juicy ... hey! Where's the smallest room?

GEOF: This way.

PETER: And she went off the deep end. *[Sings as he goes. Another crash offstage.]*

HELEN *[to* GEOF*]*: You'd better go with him or Lord knows where he'll end up.

GEOF: I hope the landlady hasn't heard him.

HELEN: Cigarette?

JO: No. Yes, I will. I'll keep it for Geof.

HELEN: You'd better have the whole bloody packet if you're in such a state.

JO: Well, he couldn't hold it any more, could he?

HELEN: No one could hold that much.

JO: How long has he been like this?

HELEN: What does that boy friend of yours do for a living?

JO: He's an art student. I suppose that's what's been keeping you occupied?

HELEN: An art student. I might have known. Does he live here?

JO: Why should I answer your questions? You never answer any of mine.

HELEN: Look at you! Why don't you take a bit of pride in yourself? Grow your hair properly?

JO: Look at you. Look what your pride in yourself has done for you.

HELEN: Come and stay with me, Jo; there's a nice room and plenty of food.

JO: No, thanks.

HELEN: You prefer to stay in this hole with that pansified little freak?

GEOF: Shall I go?

HELEN: I didn't know you'd come.

JO: Would you go and live with her if you were me, Geof?

GEOF: No, I don't think I would.

JO: Neither would anybody in their right mind.

GEOF: She always said you were a pretty rotten sort of woman. I thought she was exaggerating.

HELEN: Look, can't you get it into your stupid head that I'm offering you a decent home?

[PETER *enters, more sober, more unpleasant.]*

PETER: Bloody cockroaches are playing leapfrog in there.

HELEN: Look, I'll tell you again, in front of him, my home is yours.

PETER: Ah! Shut up!

HELEN: I'll take care of you and see you through it.

JO: The time to have taken care of me was years ago, when I couldn't take care of myself.

HELEN: All right, but we're talking about here and now. When I really set out to take care of somebody I usually do the job properly.

JO: So I see.

PETER: I'm not having that bloody slut at our place. I'll tell you that for nothing.

HELEN: Take no notice. The house is half mine.

PETER: Like hell it is. I could throw you out tomorrow.

JO: I don't think …

PETER: And don't bring that little fruitcake parcel either! *[Mumbles.]* I can't stand the sight of him. Can't stand 'em at any price.

HELEN: Oh, keep out of it. Jo, I can't bear to think of you sitting here in this dump!

PETER: Neither can I. Now let's get going.

HELEN: The whole district's rotten, it's not fit to live in.

PETER: Let's go before we grow old sitting here.

HELEN: Shut up, the pubs will be open in ten minutes.

PETER: You're wrong there. *[Looking at his watch.]* They're open now. What time do you make it?

GEOF: There's one thing about this district, the people in it aren't rotten. Anyway, I think she's happier here with me than in that dazzling white house you're supposed to be so …

PETER: Dazzling bunch of bul … lot of bloody outsiders, no class at all. What's the time anyway?

HELEN *[to GEOF]*: You shut up. I know what she needs if she's not going to finish up in a box.

PETER: What's the time by your watch, sonny?

GEOF: It's never been right since it last went wrong.

PETER: Neither have I. How long are we going to sit around in this room? I don't like the smell of unwashed bodies, woman. I dragged you out of the gutter once. If you want to go back there it's all the same to me. I'm not having this shower at any price. I'm telling you for the last time because I'm getting out of it. Stay if you want, it's all the same to me; it's your own bloody level. Well, are you coming or not?

HELEN: I'm not.

PETER: I said are you coming?

HELEN And I said I'm not.

PETER: Well, you can just go and take a flying flip out of the window. *[He goes.]*

HELEN: I'll … I'll … would you sooner I stayed here with you?

JO: No, thanks.

PETER: Helen … *[Calling]* … come on!

HELEN: I'll send you some money.

JO: Keep it. You might need it.

PETER: Helen!

HELEN: Go to …

PETER: Are you coming?

HELEN *[yelling]:* Yes. *[To GEOF.]* See that she goes to the clinic regularly and be sure she gets enough to eat.

GEOF: She has been doing that.

HELEN: I'll see you around. *[She goes.]*

JO: Well, here endeth the third lesson.

GEOF: At least she left you some money. We can get some …

JO: He took it back. I got you a cigarette though, love.

GEOF: Oh, smashing! I was out.

[Music. They dance together. Fade out.]

My Mother Said I Never Should

Act 1
Scene Four

Raynes Park, London, May 1969. The garden of KEN *and* MARGARET's *suburban semi.* JACKIE *is nearly 18, wears flared jeans with sewn-on badges;* MARGARET *is 38, wears a flowered apron and carries a tea towel. Jackie has her red transistor which blares, 'All You Need is Love'. She sprawls on the grass beside the cherry tree, next to the swing.* MARGARET *follows, flustered.*

MARGARET: *(switches off the transistor)* I should never have let you go to that party in Hammersmith!

JACKIE: Please, Mummy, leave me alone.

MARGARET: You said you were staying with his parents!

JACKIE: We were. But they didn't mind us sleeping together. Not everyone has your hang ups.

MARGARET: Oh you can wound me sometimes, Jackie!

JACKIE: You sound like Granny now.

MARGARET: What am I going to tell Daddy?

Margaret (Sheila Reid) and Jackie (Jane Gurnett), at the Royal Court, 1989.

JACKIE: If you want me to behave like an adult, then stop treating me like a child!

MARGARET: *(pause)* You don't know what might happen.

JACKIE: I might fall in love.

MARGARET: *(trying to ignore this)* You can get pregnant the first time, you know.

JACKIE: Thanks for telling me now.

MARGARET: Well if you'd come to me and said —

JACKIE: Well I did say I wanted to have a talk with you, actually, and you said 'Tell me while we go round the garden centre', don't you remember? *(Slight pause.)* Anyway, you can't scare me, because I'm on the pill, OK?

MARGARET: Since when?

JACKIE: Since before Neil and I went away at half term. You knew that because you've been reading my diary.

MARGARET: *(momentarily caught)* Well I've no idea, you might be on drugs, anything! *(Collects herself.)* I know I'm going to sound like an old fuddy duddy … but… *(Stuck.)* It's a serious step you've taken, you've no idea —

JACKIE: It was no big deal. It was a relief to get it over with. I cried afterwards. Then I laughed. I expect it's better with someone you're in love with.

MARGARET: You could have waited.

JACKIE: Why?

MARGARET: I had to.

JACKIE: That's it, isn't it? *(Gets up and goes to the house.)*

MARGARET: If this affects your A-levels!

JACKIE: *(stops)* What?

Silence. MARGARET *has nothing to say.*

JACKIE: I'm going to make a phone call. Phone Neil. *(Goes into the house.)*

MARGARET: *(pause. Picks up* JACKIE's *transistor)* I had an admirer. He took me to dinner. I'd never eaten oysters before. — Wouldn't let me see the bill, that sort of man. I was sure Ken could tell, when I got in. I'd had my hair done, on a Wednesday. *(Pause.)* Ten years ago.

Blackout.

Scene Five

Cheadle Hulme, Manchester, 1961 as in Scene Two. JACKIE *is 9,* MARGARET *is 30,* DORIS *is 61. The garden. Sound of lawnmower off right.*

DORIS *enters with a chair and a rug, and arranges them on the grass. She glares, off right.*

DORIS *(calls to right)* Jack! JACK!

The lawnmower sound stops.

DORIS: Are you coming to have tea with us? Ken and Margaret can't stop long.

Pause. The lawnmower sound starts up again. She shouts.

Well you'd better do round the front, I don't want grass clippings in our tea. *(As the lawnmower fades away to right.)* And mind my lily of the valley! *(She goes back to the house for the tea tray.)*

Enter JACKIE *leading* MARGARET *by the hand, followed by* DORIS.

JACKIE: And I've been doing the pear tree. Look. *(She shows* MARGARET *the painting.)*

MARGARET: Oh that's lovely darling!

JACKIE: Grandad let me use his real paints.

DORIS: He's been teaching you, hasn't he.

JACKIE: Did you know shadows are purple?

DORIS: Have you said hello properly?

JACKIE: *(hugs* MARGARET*)* Are you better?

MARGARET: Better? *(Looks at* DORIS.*)* Mother.

JACKIE: Where's Daddy?

MARGARET: He's gone to fill up the car with petrol.

DORIS: That chair's for you.

MARGARET: No, really.

DORIS: The rug will do quite nicely for me. *(Sits.)* Sit down and have some tea.

MARGARET: Oh we mustn't, I said to Ken we'd be ready to leave as soon as he comes back.

DORIS: Her bag is packed and in the hall.

MARGARET: If we stay for tea we won't get home to London till way past Jackie's bedtime.

JACKIE: I don't mind.

DORIS: Jackie made the cakes. Didn't you dear? *Pause.* MARGARET *gives in to pressure and sits.*

MARGARET: All right Mother. And what have you been doing, darling?

JACKIE: I broke a cup and then we broke two jam jars.

MARGARET: Oh dear.

DORIS: Jackie's been an angel.

JACKIE: *(offering the cake)* Have the yellow one with the smartie.

DORIS: I hope you've been taking the iron tablets, dear.

MARGARET: *(resists temptation to answer back. To* JACKIE, *for the cake)* Thank you.

JACKIE: *(says grace in French, very fast)* Que Dieu benisse notre pain quotidien. Amen. *(Pause.)*

MARGARET: Well this is very nice.

DORIS: And how was Windermere? Did you drive about much?

MARGARET: We stayed in a lovely guest house, a bit pricey but Ken insisted I was pampered.

JACKIE: What's pampered?

DORIS: Nursed.

Pause. JACKIE *looks at* MARGARET. MARGARET *looks at* DORIS.

MARGARET: No, pampered is — being spoiled a bit — like you've been, here!

DORIS: Thank you, Margaret.

MARGARET: And I brought you some Kendal mint cake! *(Gives it to* JACKIE.*)*

JACKIE: And some for Granny? Never mind Granny, we can share this. *(Breaks it in half and gives half to* DORIS, *then goes back to her painting.)*

DORIS: I hope you didn't do too much walking.

MARGARET: It rained a lot. Luckily there was a nice lounge with a fire. Time to sit and think. You know, Mother, I thought I didn't want it, till I lost it. *(Pause.)* It's been a blessing, you taking Jackie for the week. But I missed you, darling!

JACKIE: *(goes and hugs* MARGARET*)* I cried the first night, didn't I Granny, then at breakfast Grandad let me have your old napkin ring.

MARGARET: *(holds her)* Oh Jackie.

JACKIE: And your doll. It's like a real baby, it's got real curled up toes and fingers. I was practising. I bathed it and put it to sleep, and it shut its eyes.

MARGARET: No! *(Gets up.)*

JACKIE: Mummy —

DORIS: Jackie — *(Catches hold of her.)*

JACKIE: I didn't break her, I didn't break the doll!

DORIS: *(comforts)* Ssh ssh —

JACKIE: You're hurting! *(Breaks free and runs off, knocking the paint pot across the painting.)*

DORIS: If you hadn't been so hasty to get that temping job, you would never have lost the baby.

MARGARET: *(busying herself with the painting)* It'll dry in the evening sun, it'll be all right.

DORIS: That's for Jack. He wanted something from his grandchild.

Doris takes the painting.

Blackout.

Scene Six

A council flat on the Hulme estate, Manchester, early December 1971. JACKIE *is 19,* ROSIE *is 3 months,* MARGARET *is 40. A worn piece of rusty red carpet with ashtrays and mugs strewn on it, also the red transistor from Scene Four, now worn and battered, blares out over* ROSIE's *crying. A Moses basket of blankets represents* ROSIE; *the actress playing* ROSIE *can be seen making the sounds of the baby crying. As the lights rise,* JACKIE *is packing baby clothes into a holdall.*

RADIO *(Manchester DJ):* … Today's highest temperature is expected to be a cold 3°, so wrap up warm. Most roads in the city have been cleared now, but there's still ice and snow on the Pennines, and the forecast is more snow tonight. Police are asking motorists leaving Manchester on Northbound routes to drive slowly because of black ice. Meanwhile, here's something to remind you of summer days ('Honky Tonk Woman'.)

JACKIE: *(packing hurriedly)* I wanted it to look nice and now it won't all go in!

Rosie yells.

JACKIE: *(hits transistor, which goes off)* Ssh, Rosie, please —

Rosie yells.

JACKIE: Shut up!

Rosie stops crying abruptly.

JACKIE: *(gently)* Ssh, ssh, there now … Where do you get the energy from, yelling all night? *(Bends over Moses basket, sings haphazard tune.)* My little rabbit, in your little basket …

Rosie coos.

JACKIE: Sleep, beautiful … ssh …

ROSIE *makes a little cry as* JACKIE *moves away to pack again.*

JACKIE: *(bends over Rosie again)* Please don't be crying when Mummy and Daddy arrive! — Where's your red sock? *(Picks it up and dangles it over* ROSIE, *who quietens during:)* Look, it fell out! Give me a smile — yes! There. I even washed your red sock. Washed everything, don't want Mummy to think — *(Holding back tears.)* I've got to clear up, Rosie.

— All these ashtrays, Sandra and Hugh last night, they never think about you, do they? *(Picks up ashtray.)*

MARGARET: *(from off)* Hello?

JACKIE: Oh shit, the mess — Come in!

MARGARET: *(entering)* Hello Jackie.

JACKIE: *(immediately casual)* Hi Mummy.

MARGARET: It's not locked!

JACKIE: I knew it would be you.

MARGARET: You've been smoking.

JACKIE: Journey from London OK?

MARGARET: Not how I remembered, Mosside. All these tower blocks …

JACKIE: Is Daddy — he's not —

MARGARET: Waiting in the car.

JACKIE: He didn't mind? — I'm sorry, I couldn't face —

MARGARET: He understands.

Pause.

JACKIE: This is Rosie, Mummy.

MARGARET: I — came up the stairs. *(Pause.)* Lift is out of order. *(Pause.)* Lot of stairs.

JACKIE: … Please.

MARGARET: *(long pause)* Three months.

JACKIE: Say hello.

MARGARET: *(goes to the Moses basket. Pause)* Pretty.

JACKIE: *(goes also)* You think so?

MARGARET: You had curly eyelashes like that.

JACKIE: *(pleased)* Did I?

MARGARET: Hello Rosie … *(Kisses her.)*

JACKIE: Don't wake her!

MARGARET: Of course not!

JACKIE: I'm sorry, it's just —

MARGARET: You think I don't know?

Rosie coos quietly.

MARGARET: *(very tenderly)* Ssh, there now.

Rosie murmurs.

JACKIE: *(turns away)* I've packed her things … here. *(Gives* MARGARET *the holdall.)* And her bottles are in this carrier. There's a bit of powdered milk left —

MARGARET: Oh you really don't need —

JACKIE: Well what would I do with it?

Awkward pause. MARGARET *looks through the clothes in the holdall.*

MARGARET: I've been to Mothercare. Got some of those new disposable nappies, like you said. Quite different from when you were a baby. *(Sees another carrier, goes to pick it up.)* What about this bag — what a sweet — won't she want this dress with the rabbit on?

JACKIE: Leave those! — Things she's grown out of.

MARGARET: Why did you have to try! All by yourself! Didn't you believe me?

JACKIE: I wanted to see if our theories worked … *(Pause.)* But when I came back from hospital everyone had cleared out. You'd think I had VD, not a new baby.

MARGARET: He should be here with you, your — *(Stuck for word.)* — Rosie's father. — You in these flats …

JACKIE: *(calm)* Mummy, I told you. He visits; and sends money. It was my decision.

MARGARET: Yes but you had no idea! I told you, I told you! Nothing, for nearly three months, nothing, since the day she was born, then a phone call, out of the blue; the potatoes boiled dry!

JACKIE: You knew I'd phone, one day. *(Slight pause.)*

MARGARET: Look at you now, a year ago you had everything, you were so excited about the art school, new friends, doing so well —

JACKIE: *(angry)* I'll go back! Yes I will, finish the degree, I won't fail both things! Only think about her at night, her cheek against mine, soft and furry, like an apricot.

Rosie makes a snuffling noise in her sleep.

JACKIE: … She'll be happy, won't she?

MARGARET: After you phoned … after you asked us … Daddy went upstairs and got your old high chair down from the attic.
(Pause.) Like sisters, he said. A new little sister… *(Bends down to* ROSIE.*)* Aren't you, precious?

JACKIE: *(panics)* Mummy — she's got to know — I can't come and visit, with her not knowing, I can't!

MARGARET: Jackie, darling, we can't go over this again — you know as well as I do it would be impossible —

JACKIE: I don't believe you!

MARGARET: When she's grown up, you can tell her; when she's sixteen.

JACKIE: It'll be too late!

Silence.

Give me back the bags.

MARGARET: *(gently)* You've got such opportunities.

JACKIE: Expectations.

MARGARET: Yes!

JACKIE: Yours.

MARGARET: You've got to —

JACKIE: Why? *(Pulls away holdall.)* Why not just Rosie?

MARGARET: You've got to go further than me — and Rosie too. *(Quietly.)* Otherwise … what's it been worth?

JACKIE: *(pause)* Here, take them. *(Gives Margaret the bags.)* You haven't told Granny and Grandad?

MARGARET: Not yet. I'll talk to them. *(Tentative.)* Perhaps you could stay with them, just till Christmas, while you find a new flat?
(Bends to Rosie.) My little lamb … What's this?

JACKIE: She has to have a red sock to go to sleep.

MARGARET: You keep one.

JACKIE: *(puts one sock in her pocket)* Love her for me …

MARGARET: *picks up the Moses basket.*

JACKIE: I'll help you to the car.

MARGARET: It's all right, Daddy will be there. (MARGARET *picks up the bags. As she goes to the door.)*

JACKIE: I'll come for Christmas. And visit, lots. *(Pause.)* Whenever I can afford the fare to London.

MARGARET *exits.*

JACKIE: *(calls after them)* Sing to her at bathtime, especially the rabbit song … *(Silence. Pause. She picks up the bag she told* MARGARET *to leave. As she pulls out the clothes, she is suddenly hysterically happy. She holds up the rabbit dress.)* — Wore this the day you first smiled, you wouldn't let go of my hair, — do you remember? *(Holds up another.)* — And your first bonnet … *(Gentle.)* And the shawl … wrapped you up, like a parcel, the day we left hospital; all the way back in a taxi, bringing you home … *(Pause.)* Our secrets, Rosie. I'll take care of them. *(Pause.)* You'll never call me 'Mummy'. *(Silence. Screams.)* Rosie! Come back! Mummy, Mummy!

Blackout. For a moment in the darkness, the sound of a baby crying. In a dim light we see MARGARET *rocking a bundle. She comforts the baby with the following words, until the baby quietens and coos:*

MARGARET: There now, there now, hush! Did you have a nasty dream? My precious. Mummy's here now. Mummy's here, Rosie. There now … Did you have a bad dream, Jackie? It's all right. Ssh … ssh …

As the lights come up bright for the next scene, MARGARET *turns and billows out the sheet which was forming the bundle.*

Understanding action and structure

A Taste of Honey

Jo has found herself pregnant after a brief, passionate affair. Her mother, who is described in the first scene as a 'semi-whore', has recently married a younger man, Peter, and has been out of touch with Jo for some time. Geof, a young homosexual man, has befriended Jo. As the extract begins, Geof has persuaded Jo that he should stay and care for her and her baby.

● Why do you think Geof doesn't want Jo to know that he asked Helen to visit?

What is shown in the following extract?

> JO: Get out of here. I won't go out if I don't want to. It's nothing to do with you. Get back to your fancy man or your husband, or whatever you like to call him. [HELEN *begins to chase her.]* Aren't you afraid he'll run off and leave you if you let him out of your sight?

The play is very well structured in two acts that match each other. Both acts feature conversations between Jo and Helen, Helen's relationships with men and Jo's relationship with men (the Boy in Act 1 and Geof in Act 2).

My Mother Said I Never Should

Jackie is a young woman beginning to rebel against her parents and trying to make her way in the world. She has challenged her mother Margaret's attitudes by becoming sexually active. Later she becomes pregnant and has a child. However, Jackie is unable to lead the life she wants and calls upon her mother to help out. The story moves between past and present and the scenes tell a story that spans nearly half a century.

- In Scene 4, what is Margaret's main objection to the fact that Jackie has admitted to having sex with her boyfriend?
- In Scene 5, what arrangement is being made between Margaret and Jackie?

Keatley's structure is much more challenging (or difficult) than Delaney's because she has so many scenes in her play, although the whole of Act 2 has only one scene. What Keatley is able to do with this structure is to cover a great deal of time: the action of the play begins in 1940 and is completed in 1987.

Understanding character

A Taste of Honey

The characters in *A Taste of Honey* are:

Jo	a teenage girl
Helen	her mother
Peter	Helen's boyfriend, later husband
Boy	Jo's fiancée
Geof	A friend of Jo's

The play is, however, focused almost entirely on Jo, as she is in nearly every scene. Her character is the one the audience sympathises with most and she enables us to judge the other characters in the play. She clearly has a very stormy relationship with her mother.

- What feelings does Helen have for Jo?
- What feelings does Jo have for her mother?
- What is your view of Geof?
- What is Peter's view of Geof?

My Mother Said I Never Should

Keatley's play looks at the life of four characters:

Doris Partington	Margaret's mother
Margaret Bradley	Jackie's mother
Jackie Metcalfe	Rosie's mother
Rosie Metcalfe	

However, it is the way in which Jackie gives up her young daughter to be brought up by her mother Margaret that is the real focus of the play.

- What does the following tell us about Jackie and Margaret's relationship?

> MARGARET: Look at you now, a year ago you had everything, you were so excited about the art school, new friends, doing so well —
> JACKIE: *(angry)* I'll go back! Yes I will, finish the degree, I won't fail both things! Only think about her at night, her cheek against mine, soft and furry, like an apricot.

Understanding themes

A Taste of Honey

Shelagh Delaney presents the audience with her issues through characters who are predominantly working-class, especially Jo and Helen. She looks closely at:

sexual behaviour in adults and teenagers

single parenthood

growing up

leaving home

friendship.

The issue of single parenthood has been a very important one in the UK. It has the highest rates of child teenage pregnancy and of single mothers in western Europe. Recently stories in the press about mothers of 12 and 13 years of age have added to the debate, as has the treatment of the topic in television soap opera such as *Coronation Street*.

- How effective is Delaney's presentation of the problem in this extract?

My Mother Said I Never Should

Charlotte Keatley was writing almost thirty years after Shelagh Delaney and she was interested more in the relationships between women and the impact that children can have on women's lives. The main themes she covers are:

family relationships

the importance of the past

work and motherhood

love and sex

single parenthood

growing up.

- What do you think Doris is hinting at in the following?

DORIS: If you hadn't been so hasty to get that temping job, you would never have lost the baby.

Comparing the texts

The themes of both texts cover similar aspects of life, but are still quite different. It is interesting to look at a specific section to see these similarities and differences.

Look at the following lines from *A Taste of Honey* on page 75:

'HELEN: You couldn't wait could you? …'

down to

'JO: I wish you had done. You did with plenty of others, I know.'

Now look at the following lines from *My Mother Said I Never Should* on page 81:

'MARGARET: You could have waited.'

down to

'JACKIE: I'm going to make a phone call. Phone Neil. *(Goes into the house)*'

- Compare what is said in each passage by drawing a line down the middle of a sheet of paper and writing notes on the following:
  a) ideas about sex
  b) characters' attitudes to each other
  c) the language used.
- What similarities have you found and what differences?

Understanding dramatic devices

A Taste of Honey

Conflict

All the characters in this extract are in conflict with other characters. Characters trade insults and threats as well as trying to take control of each other. There is also an interesting conflict between the two male characters.

- Find three examples of conflict from the extract.

Humour

Shelagh Delaney was considered to be a very fresh and humorous writer and there is an energy about her writing that is still very evident forty years after the first performance. The humour is mainly verbal and stems as much from insult and sarcasm as it does from jokes. When Helen calls Geof 'Romeo' in the opening of the extract she is mocking his sexuality in a sarcastic way that is also, to some extent, humorous.

- Find three more examples of humorous speech in this extract.

Language

In the 1950s it was not possible for playwrights to use language with the full range and freedom that they now have. Therefore, the language of Delaney's play is an attempt to create a sense of working-class English without resorting to explicit obscenity.

- Find three examples of 'slangy' language in the extract, and suggest how they might be represented today.

My Mother Said I Never Should

Time

Charlotte Keatley uses time very effectively. Scene 5, as you have already noticed, is set eight years before Scene 4. This jumping between time zones makes the audience feel as if, as Keatley herself says, 'all past time is present inside us'. Keatley also believes that time is different for women, that 'time is always running out for women'. Why do you think she says this?

Language

Charlotte Keatley has written, 'Language used in *My Mother Said I Never Should* are for lies, secrets, spells, and for not saying what one means.' This is shown very well in the last speech of Margaret in Scene 4.

- What 'secret' is being revealed here?

Understanding performance

A Taste of Honey

Acting

Both male parts in this extract are worth a closer look. Geof is an effeminate character and must be played in that way to make the sarcastic remarks of Helen and Peter believable. Also, there is a wonderful 'drunk' in the figure of Peter. He sings, falls over and generally makes a real nuisance of himself, as well as appearing quite threatening towards the end of the extract.

Look at the following:

> PETER: Go on, have your blasted family reunion, don't mind me! *(Notices GEOF again)* Who's this? Oh, of course! Where are the drinks, Lana? *(He falls into the kitchen, singing)* "Getting to know you, getting to know all about you ..."

- Now read it aloud in the following way:

  a) cheerful

  b) aggressive

  c) nasty

- Which works best?

My Mother Said I Never Should

Setting

Charlotte Keatley writes in the cast list of the play: 'The setting should not be naturalistic. The design should incorporate certain objects which remain on stage throughout, such as the piano in Act One and Two, a tub of geraniums, a patch of wasteground. There are no sofas in this play. The setting should simply be a magic place where things can happen.'

- Look closely at the stage directions for Scenes 4 and 5 and the use of props.

- What is the importance of the following:

  a) the lawnmower?

  b) the transistor?

  c) Margaret's tea towel?

  d) Doris's rug?

Tasks

Personal response: writing

1   Write a short scene in which Terry, a 16-year-old boy who has just discovered that his girlfriend is pregnant, is speaking to his parents. You will need to consider:

   a) the reactions of the characters

   b) the issues they discuss

   c) attitudes to Terry's girlfriend.

2   In what ways do *A Taste of Honey* and *My Mother Said I Never Should* deal with women's lives?

   You should write about:

   a) events that affect women

   b) characters

   c) how women relate to each other

   d) how women relate to men.

Practical activities

Individually

3   *My Mother Said I Never Should* is based on the idea of key events in a person's life. Write down the four key events of your life so far.

In groups

4   Bring in an article of clothing or a piece of fabric, a hat or a brooch and prepare to speak briefly about what you think it will tell you about the wearer. (Don't bring in something of your own!)

5   Try to write a scene about a father and son where there is a crucial issue to be explored. You might want to consider:

a) a son joining the army

b) the son needing to borrow money

c) failing exams at school.

6   Allocate parts and perform each of the extracts.

Useful notes

Shelagh Delaney, *A Taste of Honey*

in your condition	pregnant
Victorian melodrama	a play with a very emotional story
organ grinder … monkey	a reference to the fact that Jo is effectively 'in charge'
Sling your hook!	Get lost! Get out of here!
a bit high	Referring to the appearance of Jo's 'bump'
came a cropper	your luck ran out
pansified freak	insulting remarks about Geof's manner
maternity benefit	a state benefit available at the time
'Little Josephine …'	From a popular song of the time
Temperance Society	an organisation to help people stay away from alcohol, like Alcoholics Anonymous
Lily	insulting reference to Geof
Mary	another insult to Geof, giving him a woman's name
Oedipus	reference to *Oedipus Rex*, a Greek tragedy
Jezebel, Cuddles	further insults to Geof
'grapefruit … bust'	Peter is bragging about sexual conquests
fruitcake	further insult to Geof
flying flip	a tame form of an obscenity
'endeth … lesson'	Jo mocks Helen's attempts to be considerate

Charlotte Keatley, *My Mother Said I Never Should*

transistor	a small radio
hang ups	a late 60s/70s term to describe concerns or worries
the pill	contraceptive pill
fuddy duddy	a fussy older person
oysters	these are meant to be aphrodisiacs, to encourage sexual desire
iron tablets	often prescribed in pregnancy
didn't want it	Margaret has had a miscarriage
Mosside	an inner city area of Manchester

Recent Social Comedy: Mike Leigh and Alan Ayckbourn

Background and context

Mike Leigh was born in Salford in 1943 and went to school there before going to the Royal Academy of Dramatic Arts (RADA) to study for the theatre. In his early days, Leigh developed a technique for writing plays that was based on improvisation. This technique has been extremely successful and Leigh has since gone on to make prize-winning films.

Leigh's work is often called 'social comedy' and is noted for its closely observed characters and language. *Abigail's Party*, which gently mocks the way people behave when they get together socially, was a hit and went on to become a very famous BBC *Play for Today* production (it is possible to obtain the video of this broadcast, with Alison Steadman heading the cast as Beverly).

Alan Ayckbourn, born in 1939, is the most successful living British playwright and he has been active in the theatre since he was seventeen years of age. He has written over fifty plays and has been knighted for his service to theatre. Most of his work has been premiered at the Stephen Joseph Theatre in Scarborough, which was named after the man who first encouraged him to write.

Ayckbourn's plays are written very much with a general, more family-type audience in mind. His work is highly amusing, but there is an undercurrent of sadness present. As a man of the theatre, Ayckbourn's plays are often very cleverly crafted, and *Absurd Person Singular* is no exception.

Abigail's Party

Act 1

[The front door bell chimes.]
BEVERLY: Would you excuse me just one minute, Ang?
 [Beverly goes out. Angela helps herself to a cheese-pineapple savoury. Meanwhile, starting offstage:]
BEVERLY: Hi, Sue.
SUSAN: Hello, Beverly.
BEVERLY: Come in.
SUSAN: Thank you.
BEVERLY: All right, Sue?
SUSAN: Yes, thank you.
BEVERLY: Come through.

SUSAN: I'm sorry I'm a bit late.

BEVERLY: Now, don't worry, Sue, that's all right. Would you like to slip your jacket off?

SUSAN: Oh, thank you.

BEVERLY: Everything all right, Sue?

SUSAN: Yes, I think so. I hope so.

BEVERLY: Come through and say hello. Ang: this is Sue. Sue, this is Ang.

ANGELA: Hello.

SUSAN: How d'you do.

BEVERLY: Sue's from Number 9.

ANGELA: Oh, we've just moved into Number 16.

SUSAN: Oh, really?

BEVERLY: Yeah, you know the Macdonalds' old house, Sue?

SUSAN: Yes.

BEVERLY: Yeah. Sit down, Sue. I'll just pop your coat in the hall. *[Going]* Won't be a sec. Make yourself at home, Sue!

SUSAN: Thank you. *[She puts a wrapped bottle on the bar, and proceeds to sit down.]*

ANGELA: We've only been here a fortnight.

SUSAN: Oh, really?

[Beverly returns.]

BEVERLY: Did you bring that, Sue?

SUSAN: Yes.

BEVERLY: Is it for us?

SUSAN: Yes.

BEVERLY: Oh, thank you, Sue!

SUSAN: It's nothing very special, I'm afraid.

BEVERLY: Ah. Isn't that kind, Ang?

ANGELA: Yes.

SUSAN: Not at all.

BEVERLY *[Unwrapping the bottle]:* Oh, lovely! 'Cos Laurence likes a drop of wine, actually. Oh, it's Beaujolais. Fantastic! Won't be a sec, I'll just pop it in the fridge. *[She goes to kitchen.]*

ANGELA: I'm so pleased to meet you. I want to meet all the neighbours.

SUSAN: Yes.

[Beverly returns.]

BEVERLY: Now, Sue: what would you like to drink?

SUSAN: I'll have a glass of sherry, please.

BEVERLY: Sherry, are you sure?

SUSAN: Yes. Thank you.

BEVERLY: 'Cos we've got everything. There's gin, whisky, vodka, brandy, whatever you'd like. Would you like a little gin-and-tonic, Sue? 'Cos me and Ang are drinking gin-and-tonic, actually.

SUSAN: All right — thank you.

BEVERLY: Ice and lemon?

SUSAN: Yes, please.

BEVERLY: Great.

ANGELA: It's a nice drink, gin-and-tonic, isn't it?

Janine Duvitski, John Salthouse, Alison Steadman and Thelma Whiteley in a production at the Hampstead Theatre, 1977.

SUSAN: Yes, it is.

ANGELA: Refreshing. *[Tony returns during:]* Sometimes I drink lager-and-lime. Say I'm in a pub with my husband, I'll drink that. But I prefer this.

TONY: Can I wash me hands, please?

BEVERLY: Yes, just one second, Tone, while I finish making Sue's drink. Sorry: Sue — this is Tony.

ANGELA: My husband.

SUSAN ⎫
TONY ⎭ : How d'you do.

ANGELA: Did you push it all right?

TONY: Yeah. The battery was flat.

BEVERLY: Sue!

SUSAN: Thank you.

BEVERLY: Cheers.

SUSAN: Oh, cheers.

BEVERLY: Now. Tony, hands! Come through. *(She takes him to kitchen)* Soap and towel there. Okay?

TONY: Ta.

ANGELA: D'you work?

SUSAN: No. No, I don't.

ANGELA: I'm a nurse.

SUSAN: Oh.

ANGELA: At St Mary's in Walthamstow.

SUSAN: Oh, yes.

ANGELA: Beverly says your daughter's having a party. Is that right?

SUSAN: That's right, yes.

ANGELA: Has it started yet?

SUSAN: Yes. Yes, it has.

BEVERLY: All right, Tone?

TONY: Yes, thank you.

BEVERLY: Come through.

[He comes through.]

Drink's on there. Like to sit down?

TONY: Ta.

BEVERLY: Now then, Sue, let's see … would you like a little cigarette?

SUSAN: Oh. No, thank you.

BEVERLY: Are you sure?

SUSAN: Yes. Thank you.

BEVERLY: Perhaps you'll have one a little bit later on. And I know Angela doesn't want one. Now, everybody all right?

TONY: Yes, thank you.

ANGELA: Yes, lovely, thanks.

SUSAN: Yes. Thank you.

BEVERLY: Yes? Great!

[Rock music starts at Number 9, not especially loud.]

BEVERLY: Aye aye! It's started, Sue.

ANGELA: They've got the record-player going, haven't they? They're going to have fun, aren't they?

BEVERLY: Sounds like it.

SUSAN: I hope so.

ANGELA: How old is she, your daughter?

SUSAN: Fifteen.

ANGELA: What does she look like? 'Cos I might have seen her.

SUSAN: Oh. Well, she's quite tall, and she's got fair hair, quite long fair hair.

ANGELA: She hasn't got a pink streak in her hair, has she?

SUSAN: Yes.

BEVERLY: Yeah, that's Abigail! And she wears those jeans, Ang, with patches on, and safety-pins right down the side, and scruffy bottoms.

ANGELA: Yes, I've seen her.

SUSAN: And plumber's overalls.

BEVERLY: Yeah, plumber's overalls. She makes me die, you know!

ANGELA: I've seen her: she was standing outside your gate with a friend. And you've seen her as well, haven't you? Getting off that motorbike.

TONY: Yeah.

ANGELA: How many people are coming to the party?

BEVERLY: About fifteen, isn't it, Sue?

SUSAN: Well, it was fifteen. Then it went up to twenty, and last night I gathered it was twenty-five.

BEVERLY: It's creeping up, Sue.

SUSAN: I've told her that's the limit. Well, I think that's enough. Don't you?

BEVERLY: Definitely, Sue, yeah, definitely.

ANGELA: Yeah.

BEVERLY: But, this is it with teenagers: okay, they tell you twenty five; but a friend invites a friend: that friend invites another friend; and it creeps up till you end up with about seventy or eighty. This is it. This is the danger!

TONY: I've just seen a couple of people arriving, actually.

SUSAN: Yes. Nice of them to help you with the car.

TONY: Oh, no — not them: a couple of coloured chaps and a girl roared up in a Ford Capri.

SUSAN: Oh, really? *[Pause.]* Well, there were only half a dozen there when I left … When I was asked to leave.

BEVERLY: Yeah, this is it, isn't it? They don't want Mum sitting there, casting a beady eye on all the goings-on, do they?

ANGELA: No. Not when they get to fifteen. When I was fifteen I really wanted a party of my own, and my Dad, he'd never let me. You see, I've got four sisters. Haven't I, Tony?

TONY: Yeah.

ANGELA: And I think he was a little bit worried that I'd invite all my friends, and they'd bring along a few of theirs, and we'd end up with a houseful.

BEVERLY: This is it.

ANGELA: And he was worried about people pinching things, and things getting broken.

BEVERLY: Have you locked your silver away, Sue?

SUSAN: No, I haven't got any. Well, not much, anyway. I've put a few things upstairs; just in case of accidents.

ANGELA: Yes, well, it's better to, isn't it? 'Cos it can easily happen.

BEVERLY: Yeah.

ANGELA: Like that egg-timer. Tony was furious. It was a wedding present.

BEVERLY: Don't get me wrong, Sue: I wasn't meaning that any of Abigail's friends are thieves — please don't think that. But, you don't know who you get at a party. And let's face it: people are light-fingered.

ANGELA: Yes.

[Pause.]

BEVERLY: D'you leave your carpets down, Sue?

SUSAN: Er — yes.

ANGELA: Have you got fitted carpets?

SUSAN: Yes.

ANGELA: Yes … we've got fitted carpets. The Macdonalds left them all. They were inclusive in the price of the house

SUSAN: Oh?

ANGELA: And we're very lucky, because we got the price of the house down from twenty-two thousand to twenty-one thousand.

SUSAN: Really.

ANGELA: I don't know what we'll do about our carpets when we have a party. 'Cos we're having a party soon, aren't we?

TONY: Housewarming.

ANGELA: Yeah. You'll have to come.

SUSAN: Thank you.

BEVERLY: This is it, though, isn't it, with fitted carpets you don't know what to do for the best. Particularly with teenagers. Because let's face it, they're not as careful as, say, we would be, d'you know what I mean, they don't think; I mean, they've got a drink in one hand, a cigarette in the other, they're having a bit of a dance, and the next thing you know is it's cigarette on your carpet, and stubbed out.

ANGELA: Is it your daughter's birthday?

SUSAN: No. She just wanted a party. No particular reason.

BEVERLY: Yeah, well, they don't need a reason these days, do they? Any excuse for a bit of a rave-up — what do they call it, freak out? D'you get that beer, Sue?

SUSAN: Yes. I got four of those big tins, and some Pomagne.

ANGELA: Oh, that's nice, isn't it?

SUSAN: Yes, it is.

BEVERLY: It's funny, at that age we used to drink Bulmer's Cider. We used to say, 'A glass of cider, and she's anybody's.'

ANGELA: I got very drunk on champagne at our wedding. D'you remember?

TONY: Yeah.

BEVERLY: Gives you a terrible headache, champagne, doesn't it?

ANGELA: Yes. In the morning.

BEVERLY: Yeah, shocking. D'you get any spirits, Sue?

SUSAN: No. No, I didn't.

BEVERLY: No. You're very wise. 'Cos they're so expensive, aren't they? And let's face it, if they want to drink spirits, they can bring their own. Particularly the older boys. 'Cos they're working, aren't they? I mean, there will be older boys at the party, won't there?

SUSAN: Oh, yes.

BEVERLY: Yeah. Well, let's face it, Ang, when you're fifteen you don't want to go out with a bloke who's fifteen, do you?

ANGELA: No.

BEVERLY: 'Cos they're babies, aren't they? I mean, when I was fifteen, I was going out with a bloke who was twenty-one.

[Pause.]

How's Abigail getting on with that bloke, by the way, Sue?

SUSAN: I'm not sure: I daren't ask.

BEVERLY: Mind you, I reckon you're better to let her go out with as many blokes as she wants to at that age, rather than sticking to the one. Don't you agree with me, Ang?

ANGELA: Yes. How many boyfriends has she got?

SUSAN: I don't know. I don't think she really knows herself.

ANGELA: Footloose and fancy free!

BEVERLY: Actually, Sue, I was just thinking: it might be a good idea if a little bit later on, if Laurence and Tony pop down there. Now I don't mean go in; but, just to check that everything's all right; put your mind at rest. Don't you agree with me, Ang?

ANGELA: Yes, it's a good idea. You don't mind do you?

TONY: No.

SUSAN: It's very nice of you. But I don't think it'll be necessary.

TONY: Your husband's away, then, is he?

SUSAN: No. We've split up, actually.

ANGELA: Are you separated, or divorced?

SUSAN: Divorced.

ANGELA: When did you get divorced?

SUSAN: Three years ago.

ANGELA: Oh, well: that's given you time to sort of get used to it, hasn't it? We've been married three years — three years in September, isn't it?

BEVERLY: Yeah, me and Laurence have been married three years, actually.

ANGELA: Oh, it's funny — we were all getting married about the same time as you were getting divorced!

SUSAN: What a coincidence.

Absurd Person Singular

Act 2

GEOFFREY *and* EVA JACKSON'S *kitchen in their fourth-floor flat.*
This Christmas.
One door leads to the sitting-room, another into a walk-in cupboard.
The room gives an immediate impression of untidiness. It is a room continually lived in, unlike the HOPCROFTS' *immaculate ship's bridge. While it gives signs that the owners have a certain taste for the trendy homespun in both equipment and furnishing; some of the equipment, particularly the gas stove, has seen better days. Besides the stove, the room contains a table (natural scrubbed wood), kitchen chairs (natural scrubbed wood), a chest of drawers (natural scrubbed wood) and a fridge and sink.*
When the CURTAIN *rises* EVA, *unmade-up, unkempt and baggy-eyed, sits at the table in her dressing-gown. She is writing with a stub of pencil in a notepad. Whatever it is, it is difficult to word. She and the floor around her are ringed with screwed-up pieces of paper. In front of her is an open scotch bottle. After a minute she tears out the page she has been working on, screws that up as well, and tosses it on the floor to join the others. She starts again.*
A door slams. From the sitting-room comes the sound of a large dog barking. EVA *looks up alarmed, consults her watch, gives a moan, and quickly closes the notepad to cover up what she has been writing.* GEOFFREY'S *voice is heard off.*

GEOFFREY *[off]:* Darling? Eva — Eva! Quiet, George!

    [GEOFFREY *backs in from the sitting-room.*]

    [GEORGE *is still barking with with glee.*]

George! That's enough, George! Don't be silly, boy. Sit, George. Sit, boy. At once. That's a good boy. Sit. Good George. Good...

    [GEORGE *has quietened.* GEOFFREY *goes to close the door.*

    GEORGE *barks with fresh vigour.*]

George...! *[Giving up]* Oh, all right, suit yourself. *[He closes the door, turning to face* EVA *for the first time.]* Hallo, darling. *[He gives her a kiss as he passes.]*

    [EVA *hardly seems to notice. Instead, she sits fiddling with one of her pieces of screwed-up paper. Her face is a tense blank.*]

God, I need a drink. You want a drink? *[Without waiting for a reply, he takes the scotch, finds a glass and pours himself a drink.]* You want one? No? *[He puts the bottle back on the table and drinks.]* Cheers. I think we're running into some sort of trouble with the Harrison job. Helluva day. Would you believe I could spend two months explaining to them exactly how to assemble that central-dome. I go along this morning, they're trying to put a bloody great pillar up the middle, straight through the fountain. I said to them, 'Listen, you promise to put it up as you're told to — I promise it'll stay up, all right?' I now have to tell Harrison that, his super Shopperdrome that he thought was only going to cost so much is going to finish up at twice that. He is not going to be pleased. No, I think I'm in trouble unless I can... Oh well, what the hell, it's Christmas. *[Going to the window.]* You know, I think it's going to snow. By Boxing Day, that site'll be under six foot of slush, mark my words. That'll put us another six months behind. *[Retuning from the window.]* Why didn't I pick something simple? *[Seeing the screwed-up paper.]* What've you been up to? *[He tries to take* EVA'S *writing pad.]*

[EVA *clings to the pad.* GEOFFREY *shrugs, moves away, then turns and looks at her.]* You all right? You're still in your dressing-gown, did you know? Eva? Are you still thinking about this morning? I phoned you at lunch, you know. Were you out? Eva? Oh, come on darling, we talked it over, didn't we? We were up till four o'clock this morning talking it over. You agreed. You did more than agree. I mean, it was your idea. And you're right. Believe me, darling, you were right. We can't go on.

Sooner or later one of us has got to do something really positive for once in our lives — for both our sakes. And it's absolutely true that the best thing that could happen to you and me, at this point in our lives, is for me to go and live with Sally. You were absolutely right. You know, I was thinking on the way home — I nipped in for a quick one, that's why I'm a bit late. — I was thinking, this could actually work out terribly well. If we're adult about it, I mean. Don't behave like lovesick kids or something. Sally and I will probably get somewhere together — and by that time you'll probably have got yourself fixed up — we could still see each other, you know. What I'm really saying is, let's not go through all that nonsense — all that good-bye, I never want to see you again bit. Because I do want to see you again. I always will. I mean, five years. We're not going to throw away five years, are we? Eva? Eva, if you're sitting there blaming yourself for this in any way, don't. It's me, love, it's all me. It's just I'm — okay, I'm weak, as you put it. I'm unstable. It's something lacking in me, I know. I mean, other men don't have this trouble. Other men can settle down and be perfectly happy with one woman for the rest of their lives. And that's a wonderful thing. Do you think I don't envy that? *[Banging the table]* God, how I envy them that. I mean, do you' really think I enjoy living out my life like some sexual Flying Dutchman? Eva, please — please try and see my side just a little, will you? Look, it's Christmas Eve. The day after Boxing Day, I promise — I'll just clear everything of mine that you don't need out of the flat. That way, you can forget I even existed, if that's what you want. But can't we try, between us, to make the next couple of days… *[He breaks off]* Did I say it's Christmas Eve? Haven't we got some people coming round? Yes, surely we… What time did we ask them for?

[He looks at his watch.] Oh, my God. You didn't remember to put them off by any chance, did you? No. Well then… Have we got anything to drink in the house? Apart from this? *[He holds up the bottle of scotch.]* Oh well, we'll have that for a start. Now then… *[He finds a tray, puts it on the table and puts the scotch bottle on the table.]* What else have we got?

[He rummages in the cupboards.] Brandy. That'll do. Bottle of coke. Aha, what's this? Tonic wine? Who's been drinking tonic wine? Is that you? Eva? Oh, for heaven's sake, Eva — you've made your point, now snap out of it, will you? We have lots of people coming round who were due five minutes ago.

Now come on… *[He looks at her and sighs.]* O.K. I get the message. O.K. There is no help or co-operation to be expected from you tonight, is that it? All systems shut down again, have they? All right. All right. It won't be the first time don't worry. *[He returns to his hunt for bottles.]* I mean it's not as if you're particularly famous as a gracious hostess, is it? It hasn't been unheard of for you to disappear to bed in the middle of a party and be found later reading a book. *[Producing a couple more bottles — gin and sherry.]* I should think our friends will be a little disappointed if you do put in an appearance. *[Finding an assortment of glasses.]* When I say our friends, perhaps I should say yours. I will remind you that, so far as I can remember, all the people coming tonight come under the heading of your friends and not mine. And if I'm left to entertain them tonight because you choose to opt out, I shall probably finish up being very, very rude to them. Is that clear? Right. You have been warned. Yes, I know. You're very anxious, aren't you, that I should go and work for the up and coming Mr Hopcroft? So is up and coming Mr Hopcroft. But I can tell you both, here and now, I have no intention of helping to perpetrate his squalid little developments. What I lack in morals — I make up in ethics. [GEOFFREY *stamps out into the sitting-room with the tray.] [Off as* GEORGE *starts barking again.]* George — no, this is not for you. Get down, I said get down. *[There is a crash as of a bottle coming off the tray.]* Oh, really — this damn dog — get out of it…

[GEOFFREY *returns with a couple of old coffee-cups which he puts in the sink.]* That room is like a very untidy cesspit. *[He finds a dish cloth.]* One quick drink, that's all they're getting…Then it's happy Christmas and out they bloody well go.

    [GEOFFREY *goes out again. He takes with him the dish cloth.]*

    [EVA *opens her notepad and continues with her note.]*

    [GEOFFREY *returns. He still has the cloth. In the other hand he has a pile of bits of broken dog biscuit.]*

Half-chewed biscuit. Why does he only chew half of them, can you tell me that? *[He deposits the bits in the waste bin. He is about to exit again, then pauses.]* Eva? Eva — I'm being very patient. Very patient indeed. But in a minute I really do believe I'm going to lose my temper. And we know what happens then, don't we? I will take a swing at you and then you will feel hard done by and, by way of reprisal, will systematically go round and smash everything in the flat. And come tomorrow breakfast time, there will be the familiar sight of the three of us, you, me and George, trying to eat our meals off our one surviving plate. Now, Eva, please…

    [*The doorbell rings.* GEORGE *starts barking.]*

Oh, my God. Here's the first of them. *[Calling.]* George. Now, Eva, go to bed now, please. Don't make things any more embarrassing. *[As he goes out.]* George, will you be quiet.

    [GEOFFREY *goes out. The door closes. Silence.]*

    [EVA *opens her notepad, finishes her note and tears it out. She pushes the clutter on the table to one side slightly. She goes to a drawer and produces a kitchen knife. She returns to the table and pins the note forcibly to it with the knife. She goes to the window.]*

    [GEOFFREY *returns.]*

    [*Barking and chattering are heard in the background — two voices.* EVA *stands motionless, looking out.]*

[Calling back.] He's all right. He's quite harmless. Bark's worse than his bite. *[He closes the door.]* It would be the bloody Hopcrofts, wouldn't it. Didn't think they'd miss out. And that lift's broken down, would you believe it. *[Finding a bottle-opener in a drawer.]* Every Christmas. Every Christmas, isn't it? Eva, come on, love, for heaven's sake.

    [GEOFFREY *goes out, closing the door.]*

    [EVA *opens the window. She inhales the cold fresh air. After a second, she climbs uncertainly on to the window ledge. She stands giddily, staring down and clutching on to the frame.]*

    [*The door opens, chatter,* GEOFFREY *returns, carrying a glass.]*

[Calling behind him] I'll get you a clean one, I'm terribly sorry. I'm afraid the cook's on holiday. *[He laughs.]*

> *[The Hopcrofts' laughter is heard.* GEOFFREY *closes the door.]*

Don't think we can have washed these glasses since the last party. This one certainly didn't pass the Jane Hopcroft Good Housekeeping Test, anyway. *[He takes a dish cloth from the sink and wipes the glass rather casually.]* I sometimes think that woman must spend… Eva! What are you doing?

[EVA, *who is now feeling sick with vertigo, moans.]*

Eva! Eva — that's a good girl. Down. Come down — come down — that's a good girl — down. Come on… *[He reaches Eva.]*

That's it. Easy. Come on, I've got you. Down you come. That's it.

[He eases EVA *gently back into the room. She stands limply. He guides her inert body to a chair.]*

Come on, sit down here. That's it. Darling, darling, what were you trying to do? What on earth made you want to…? What was the point of that, what were you trying to prove? I mean… *[He sees the note and the knife for the first time.]* What on earth's this? *[He reads it.]* Oh, no. Eva, you mustn't think of… I mean, what do you mean, a burden to everyone? Who said you were a burden? I never said you were a burden

[During the above, EVA *picks up the bread-knife, looks at it, then at one of the kitchen drawers. She rises, unseen by* GEOFFREY, *crosses to the drawer and, half opening it, wedges the knife inside so the point sticks out. She measures out a run and turns to face the knife.* GEOFFREY, *still talking, is now watching her absently.* EVA *works up speed and then takes a desperate run at the point of the knife.* GEOFFREY, *belatedly realizing what she's up to, rushes forward, intercepts her and re-seats her.]*

Eva, now, for heaven's sake! Come on… *[He studies her nervously.]* Look, I'm going to phone the doctor. I'll tell him you're very upset and overwrought. *[He backs away and nearly impales himself on the knife. He grabs it.]* He can probably give you something to calm you down a bit.

[The doorbell rings.]

Oh God, somebody else. Now, I'm going to phone the doctor. I'll just be two minutes, all right? Now, you sit there. Don't move, just sit there like a good girl. *[Opening the door and calling off]* Would you mind helping yourselves? I just have to make one phone call…

> [GEOFFREY *goes out.]*

> *[Silence.* EVA *finishes another note. A brief one. She tears it out and weights it down, this time with a tin of dog food which happens to be on the table. She gazes round, surveying the kitchen. She stares at the oven. She goes to it and opens it, looking inside thoughtfully. She reaches inside and removes a casserole dish, opens the lid, wrinkles her nose and carries the dish to the draining-board. Returning to the oven, she removes three shelves and various other odds and ends that seem to have accumulated in there. It is a very dirty oven. She looks at her hands, now grimy, goes to the kitchen drawer and fetches a nearly clean tea towel. Folding it carefully, she lays it on the floor of the oven. She lies down and sticks her head inside, as if trying it for size. She is apparently dreadfully uncomfortable.*

> *She wriggles about to find a satisfactory position.] [The door opens quietly and* JANE *enters.]*

Eva (Jennifer Wiltsie) sits at the table, the note which she has written covered with a tin of dog food.

[The hubbub outside has now died down to a gentle murmur so not much noise filters through. JANE carries rather carefully two more glasses she considers dirty. She closes the door. She looks round the kitchen but sees no one. She crosses, rather furtively, to the sink and rinses the glasses. EVA throws an oven tray on to the floor with a clatter. JANE, startled, takes a step back and gives a little squeak. EVA, equally startled, tries to sit up in the oven and hits her head with a clang on the remaining top shelf]

JANE: Mrs Jackson, are you all right? You shouldn't be on the cold floor in your condition, you know. You should be in bed. Surely? Here…

[She helps EVA to her feet and steers her back to the table.]

Now, you sit down here. Don't you worry about that oven now. That oven can wait. You clean it later. No point in damaging your health for an oven, is there? Mind you, I know just what you feel like, though. You suddenly get that urge, don't you? You say, I must clean that oven if it kills me. I shan't sleep, I shan't eat till I've cleaned that oven. It haunts you. I know just that feeling. I'll tell you what I'll do. Never say I'm not a good neighbour — shall I have a go at it for you? How would that be? Would you mind? I mean, it's no trouble for me. I quite enjoy it, actually — and you'd do the same for me, wouldn't you? Right. That's settled. No point in wasting time, let's get down to it. Now then, what are we going to need? Bowl of water, got any oven cleaner, have you? Never mind, we'll find it — I hope you're not getting cold, you look very peaky. *[Hunting under the sink.]* Now then, oven cleaner?

Have we got any? Well, if we haven't, we'll just have to use our old friend Mr Vim, won't we? *[She rummages.]*

[The door opens. GEOFFREY enters and goes to EVA. Conversation is heard in the background.]

GEOFFREY: Darling, listen, it looks as if I've got… *[Seeing JANE.]* Oh.

JANE: Hallo, there.

GEOFFREY: Oh, hallo — anything you — want?

JANE: I'm just being a good neighbour, that's all. Have you by any chance got an apron I could borrow?

GEOFFREY *[rather bewildered, pointing to the chair]*: Er — yes — there.

JANE: Oh, yes. *[Putting it on.]* Couldn't see it for looking.

GEOFFREY: Er — what are you doing?

JANE: Getting your oven ready for tomorrow, that's what I'm doing.

GEOFFREY: For what?

JANE: For your Christmas dinner. What else do you think for what?

GEOFFREY: Yes, well, are you sure…

JANE: Don't worry about me. *[She bustles around singing loudly, collecting cleaning things and a bowl of water.]*

GEOFFREY *[over this, irritated]*: Oh. Darling — Eva, look I've phoned the doctor but he's not there. He's apparently out on a call somewhere and the fool woman I spoke to has got the address and no number. It'll be quicker for me to try and catch him there than sitting here waiting for him to come back. Now, I'll be about ten minutes, that's all. You'll be all right, will you?

JANE: Don't you fret. I'll keep an eye on her. *[She puts on a rubber glove.]*

GEOFFREY: Thank you. *[He studies the immobile EVA. On a sudden inspiration, crosses to the kitchen drawer and starts taking out the knives. He scours the kitchen, gathering up the sharp implements.]*

[JANE watches him, puzzled.]

[By way of explanation.] People downstairs are having a big dinner party. Promised to lend them some stuff.

JANE: Won't they need forks?

GEOFFREY: No. No forks. They're Muslims. *[As he goes to the door.]* Ten minutes.

   [The doorbell rings.]

JANE: There's somebody.

GEOFFREY: The Brewster-Wrights, probably.

JANE: Oh.

   [GEOFFREY goes out, the dog barking as he does so, until the door is closed.]

Hark at that dog of yours. Huge, isn't he? Like a donkey — huge. Do you know what Dick's bought him? Dick Potter?

He's bought George a Christmas present. One of those rubber rings. You know the ones you throw in the air. One of those.

He loves it. He's been running up and down your hallway out there — Dick throwing it, him trying to catch it. But he's really wonderful with dogs, Dick. He really understands them. Do you know he nearly became a dog handler only he didn't have his proper eyesight. But he knows how to treat them. Doesn't matter what sort of dog it is… He knows all their ways. *[Turning to the oven.]* Now then — oh, this is going to be a big one, isn't it? Dear oh dear. Never mind. Where there's a will. *[Removing the tea towel from the oven.]* You haven't been trying to clean it with this, have you? You'll never clean it with this. Good old elbow grease — that's the way. *[She sets to work, her head almost inside the oven.]* Shall I tell you something — Sidney would get so angry if he heard me saying this — but I'd far sooner be down here on the floor, on my knees in the oven — than out there, talking. Isn't that terrible. But I'm never at ease, really, at parties. I don't enjoy drinking, you see. I'd just as soon be out here, having a natter with you. *[She starts to sing cheerily as she works, her voice booming round the oven.]*

   [During this, EVA rises opens the cupboard, pulls out a tin box filled with first-aid things and searches through the contents.

   Eventually, she finds a white cylindrical cardboard pill box which is what she's looking for. She goes to the sink with it and runs herself a glass of water. She opens the box, takes out a couple of small tablets and puts the box back on the draining-board. She swallows one tablet with a great deal of difficulty and water. The same with the second. She leaves the tap running, pulls the cotton-wool out of the box —- and the rest of the pills rattle down the drain. EVA tries desperately to save some with her finger before they can disappear, turning off the tap. This proving ineffective, she tries with a fork.]

   [The door opens. Barking and chatting are heard. SIDNEY enters.]

SIDNEY: Halo, hallo. Where's everyone gone then… *[Seeing JANE]* Dear oh dear. I just can't believe it. I just can't believe my eyes. You can't be at it again. What are you doing?

JANE: She's under the weather. She needs a hand.

SIDNEY: Do you realize that's your best dress?

JANE: Oh, bother my best dress.

SIDNEY: Mr and Mrs Brewster-Wright have arrived, you know. Ron and Marion. I hope they don't chance to see you down there. *[Turning to* EVA *who is still fishing rather half-heartedly with the fork.]* And what's the trouble over here, eh? Can I help — since it seems to be in fashion this evening?

*[*SIDNEY *takes the fork from* EVA *and seats her in her chair.]*

Now. I'll give you a little tip, if you like. You'll never get a sink unblocked that way. Not by wiggling a fork about in it, like that. That's not the way to unblock a sink, now, is it? All you'll do that way, is to eventually take the chrome off your fork and possibly scratch the plug hole. Not the way. Let's see now … *[He runs the tap for a second and watches the water running away.]* Yes. It's a little on the sluggish side. Just a little. But it'll get worse. Probably a few tea-leaves, nothing more. Let's have a look, shall we? *[He opens the cupboard under the sink.]* Ten to one, this is where your troubles lie. Ah-ha. It's a good old-fashioned one, isn't it? Need the wrench for that one.

JANE: He'll soon fix that for you, won't you, Sidney?

SIDNEY: Brace of shakes. Shake of braces as we used to say in the Navy. I've got the tools. Down in the car. No trouble at all. *[He turns to* EVA.*]* Nothing serious. All it is, you see — where the pipe bends under the sink there - they call that the trap. Now then. *[He takes out a pencil.]* I'll show you. Always useful to know. Paper? *[He picks up* EVA'S *latest suicide note.]* This is nothing vital, is it …? Now then *[He glances curiously at it, then turns it over and starts to draw his diagram on the back.]* Now — here's your plug hole, do you see, here — if I can draw it — and this is your pipe coming straight down and then almost doubling back on itself like that, for a second, you see? Then it runs away here, to the drain…

JANE: You want to know anything, you ask Sidney…

SIDNEY: And this little bit here's the actual drain trap. And all you have to do is get it open and out it all comes. Easy when you know. Now I suppose I'll have to walk down four flights for my tools. *[He screws up the paper and throws it away. At the door.]* Now, — don't worry. Lottie's keeping them entertained at the moment and Dick's busy with George, so everybody's happy, aren't they?

> *[*SIDNEY *opens the door and goes out. We hear* LOTTIE's *laughter and the dog barking distantly for a moment before the door closes.]*

JANE: It's at times like this you're glad of your friends, aren't you? *[She goes at the oven with fresh vigour, singing cheerily.]*

> *[During the above* EVA *writes another brief note and places it in a prominent position on the table. She now rises and goes to a chair where there is a plastic washing basket filled with clean but unironed clothes. Coiled on top is a washing line. She returns to the table.* JANE, *emerging for fresh water, catches sight of her.]*

Sorting out your laundry? You're a terror, aren't you? You're worse than me. *[She returns to her oven and resumes her song.]*

> *[*EVA *begins to pull the washing line from the basket. She finds one end and ties it in a crude noose. She tests the effectiveness of this on one wrist and, satisfied, pulls the rest of the rope from the basket. Every foot or so is a plastic clothes peg which she removes.]*

I think I'm beginning to win through. I think I'm down to the metal, anyway, that's something. There's about eight layers on here.

[EVA *comes across a pair of knickers and two pairs of socks still pegged to the line. She removes these and replaces them in the basket.*]

There's something stuck on the bottom here like cement. You haven't had cement for dinner lately, have you? *[She laughs.]*

[EVA *now stands with her clothes line gazing at the ceiling. There are two light fittings and her eyes rest on the one immediately above the table. She crosses to the door, clicks a switch and just this one goes out.]*

Whooo! Where was Moses…? What's happened? Bulb gone, has it? We'll get Sidney to fix that when he comes back.

Keep him on the go. *[She returns to the oven again, changing her tune to something suitable like 'Dancing in the Dark'.]*

[EVA *climbs first on to a chair, then on to the table holding her rope. She removes the bulb and shade in one from the socket and places them on the table at her feet. She is beginning to yawn more and more frequently and is obviously beginning to feel the effect of the sleeping pills. Swaying slightly, she starts to tie the rope round the flex above the holder. This proves a difficult operation since she has far too much rope for the job. She finally manages a knot which loosely encircles the flex. She gives the rope a gentle tug — it holds. She tries again. It still remains in position. She gives it a third tug for luck. The rope slides down the flex as far as the bulb-holder and promptly pulls this away from the wires. The holder clatters on to the table and she is left clutching the rope. She stands swaying pronouncedly now, a faint look of desperation on her face.]*

[RONALD *enters. Behind him we hear* LOTTIE POTTER'S *laughter and, more distant, a dog barking.]*

RONALD: Now then, how's our little invalid getting… *[Seeing* EVA] Oh, good God. *[he dashes forward and steadies* EVA.]

My dear girl, what on earth are you doing up there?

JANE *[emerging from her oven]:* Oh, no. She's a real terror, you know. *[She goes to assist* RONALD *in helping* EVA *off the table and back on to a chair.]* She can't keep still for a minute. *[Reprovingly to* EVA.] You could have hurt yourself up there; you silly thing.

[RONALD *folds up the rope, which is looped round* EVA'S *wrist, and leaves it in her hand.]*

RONALD: Lucky! …

JANE: Yes, it was.

RONALD: I mean. What was she trying to do?

JANE: Bulb's gone.

RONALD *[looking up]:* Yes, so it has. Well, you could have asked me to do that, you know. I'm no handyman but even I can change a bulb.

[SIDNEY *enters with a large bag of tools. Behind him we hear* LOTTIE'S *laughter and a dog barking.]*

Eva (Jennifer Wiltsie) climbs on to the table holding the rope.

Understanding action and structure

Abigail's Party

Abigail's Party mocks the way in which people relate to each other in social situations. As the evening moves on and characters increasingly indulge in alcohol, they reveal a great deal about themselves and their values. Inevitably, the party ends in disaster with Beverly's husband Laurence having what appears to be a fatal heart attack. The play is cleverly structured, with plenty of 'harmless' amusement in Act 1 and unpleasantness anger and pain in Act 2 (although it is still very funny).

Look at the questions Ang ask Sue and the comments Beverly makes.

- What is Ang trying to find out about?

- What does Beverly say to make Sue uncomfortable?

Absurd Person Singular

Absurd Person Singular is a play that is built on three Christmas parties that are all, in their own way, disastrous. The parties take place over three years so the audience is able to find out about the changes to the lives of the characters that have happened in the gap between the parties. In the party we have looked at, Eva and Geoffrey are clearly going through a very difficult time and Eva's continuous attempts to kill herself are the main focus of the action.

- Find two methods that Eva uses to try to kill herself.

Look at the section on page 106 from:

'JANE: Mrs Jackson, are you all right? …'

down to

'Well, if we haven't, we'll just have to use our old friend Mr Vim, won't we?'

- What mistaken view does Jane have about Eva here?

Eva's attempts at suicide turn out to be as unsuccessful in the later parts of the play as they are in our extract, and in the last act of the play, it is Eva who seems to have the upper hand in their marriage.

Understanding character

Abigail's Party

Ang's character comes through very clearly here in the way she deals with Sue, as does Beverly's.

- Draw up a table and give a points score between 1–10 to show how appropriate each of the following words is to describe Ang and Beverly:
  a) friendly
  b) considerate
  c) nosy
  d) interfering
  e) cruel
  f) patronising.

Absurd Person Singular

The characters of Geoffrey and Eva are set on a collision course, with Eva's attempted suicide being an answer to what Geoffrey has told her about his plans for the future. Look closely at Geoffrey's opening speech and particularly the following lines on page 102 from:

'GEOFFREY: … You all right? You're still in your dressing gown…'

down to

'Did I say it's Christmas Eve? Haven't we got some people coming round? Yes, surely we…'

- What does this section tell us about Geoffrey and his attitude to Eva?

Understanding themes

Abigail's Party

Leigh's main themes are:

> foolishness
>
> pretension or 'putting on airs'
>
> the war between the sexes
>
> envy.

- Look closely at the extract to see if you can find evidence to support each of the above points.

This play has sometimes been criticised for presenting a rather cruel view of people – that they are foolish and vain, without any real values. However, his later work is more mellow and in *Secrets and Lies*, the film which won the Palme D'Or at Cannes, Leigh is extremely sympathetic to his characters.

Absurd Person Singular

Ayckbourn is sometimes described as an 'anatomist' of modern marriage. That is, he is considered to be at his best when he is looking closely and dispassionately at the institution of marriage, just like a doctor might look at a human body. In this play, he looks at three failing marriages by showing us a 'party' in each household.

- How does Ayckbourn show the audience the breakdown in communications between Geoffrey and Eva?
- Do you think it is acceptable for a writer to make an audience laugh at others' suffering, as Ayckbourn does in this extract?

Understanding dramatic devices

Abigail's Party

Mike Leigh is noted for his extremely close observation of the small things in daily life, the minutiae of existence, as they are sometimes called. Close observation is evident in *Abigail's Party*. Look closely at the following extract:

> BEVERLY: Now, Sue: what would you like to drink?
> SUSAN: I'll have a glass of sherry, please.
> BEVERLY: Sherry, are you sure?
> SUSAN: Yes. Thank you.
> BEVERLY: 'Cos we've got everything. There's gin, whisky, vodka, brandy, whatever you'd like. Would you like a little gin-and-tonic, Sue? 'Cos me and Ang are drinking gin-and-tonic, actually.
> SUSAN: All right — thank you.

- In what way is this conversation like normal speech?

Comic features

Leigh is considered to be a great comic talent, and it is sometimes said that this comedy comes from embarrassment at other people's uneasiness and misfortune. A good example of this is on page 100:

'TONY: Your husband's away, then, is he?

SUSAN: No. We've split up, actually.'

down to

'SUSAN: What a coincidence.'

- What is funny about the above conversation?

Absurd Person Singular

Dramatic irony

One of the most powerful techniques that any dramatist has at their disposal is dramatic irony. This occurs when the audience is aware of a fate in store for a character or characters, which they themselves are unaware of. This makes the audience experience very tense and often thrilling. Here, because of Ayckbourn's skill, it is also very funny.

- What does the audience know about Eva that other characters do not?

Understanding performance

Abigail's Party

Acting

Abigail's Party is tremendously funny, if played for its humorous qualities. The BBC version of the play, with Alison Steadman as Beverly, is an exceptional performance and very true to the original theatrical staging. Steadman makes Beverly into a kind of monster, through her acting style which exaggerates the irritating qualities of her behaviour.

Set

This play is performed in the same enclosed space, through two acts. As in many plays the set is very important at particular moments, but in this extract all the drama is conveyed through words alone.

Absurd Person Singular

Words, action and action 'off'

Throughout this extract and for the whole of the second Act of *Absurd Person Singular*, apart from a moment at the end when she begins to sing 'On the First Day of Christmas', Eva is silent. However, she is the focus of the audience's attention because of her actions. Her attempts at suicide are hilariously funny and very sad at the same time. Look again at the section where she tries to hang herself with the rope.

- What difficulties would a director have in making sure this episode ran well?

Another interesting aspect of this play is 'action off' (i.e. offstage).

- How are George the dog and Dick Potter used as examples of 'action off'?

Tasks

Personal response: writing

Absurd Person Singular

1   Write a short scene which is set during a party, where a group of friends talk about someone they know, only for that person to arrive a little while later. Explore in your scene the behaviour of the group of friends before and after the entrance of the other person.

2   What are your views on the relationship between Geoffrey and Eva?

You should write about:

a) what Geoffrey says

b) what Eva does

c) the way comedy is produced.

Practical activities

Individually or in pairs

Abigail's Party

3   Look at the way Beverly, Angela and Susan greet each other. Try to write a short scene where a group of male characters greet each other, bringing out the differences with Leigh's play.

4   A number of comments that are made to Sue are rather 'insensitive'. Find three such comments or questions.

Absurd Person Singular

5   Write a short scene between two characters where one character does all the talking and the other character is involved in action only. Try to think of a setting that is quite different from *Absurd Person Singular*.

6   Look closely at *Absurd Person Singular* and give three reasons why this extract could not be performed in class.

7   Using ICT you should visit the following websites to do some research into the background of these plays:

Abigail's Party

http://www.robotwisdom.com/jorn/leigh.html
http://www.tohu-bohu.com/leigh/links.html

Absurd Person Singular

http://www.webart.co.uk/clients/sjt/aa.htm
http://www.britannica.com/bcom/eb/article/idxref/6/0,5716,308886,00.html
http://playwrites.net/playwrights/1999/fjune/AlanAyckbourn1.html

In groups

8   Allocate parts for this extract of *Abigail's Party* and perform it.

Useful notes

Mike Leigh, Abigail's Party

cheese pineapple savoury	a little snack, popular in the 1970s
pop it in the fridge	normally this kind of wine would be drunk at room temperature
Tone	a familiar form of 'Tony'
Record player	to play 'vinyl' discs rather than compact discs

light-fingered	capable of theft
rave-up, freak-out	terms from the 1970s meaning 'having a party' or 'partying'
Pomagne	imitation champagne made from apples

Alan Aykbourn, *Absurd Person Singular*

homespun	everyday, put together from available materials
natural scrubbed wood	this was a fashion with middle class people in the 1970s
Harrison job	Geoffrey is an architect and Harrison is a client
Flying Dutchman	a legend about a ghostly sailor who cannot find land, made into an opera by Richard Wagner
up and coming	somebody on the way up (in terms of job or money)
squalid	seedy and disreputable
Brace of shakes	two shakes (i.e. in a short time)

An African Satire: *Jero's Metamorphosis* by Wole Soyinka

Background and context

Nobel Prize winner Wole Soyinka was born in Abeokuta, in Eastern Nigeria in 1934. His father was headmaster of a primary school and his mother was a shop owner. After completing studies in Nigeria, he went on to study at the University of Leeds in England, where he got involved in student theatre. As a writer he has often found himself in trouble with the Nigerian authorities and he went to prison for two years in the 1960s.

Soyinka's work is always interesting and imaginative, despite the fact that his plays deal directly with political issues. *Jero's Metamorphosis* is no exception, and the play very cleverly mocks the military government in Nigeria. His approach in this play is to create a play that can be linked directly to events in the outside world (sometimes called an allegory); the questionable goings-on of Jero represent the way in which Nigeria, as a country, was being run at that time.

In 1986, Soyinka won the Nobel Prize for Literature, the first black African to do so. However, he is still a very controversial figure in Nigeria where he has campaigned tirelessly for democracy and civil rights.

Jero's Metamorphosis

Scene 3

The front space of BROTHER JERO's *headquarters. Loud chatter among a most bizarre collection of prophets.* SISTER REBECCA *emerges from the house carrying the portrait from the office and hangs it against the outer wall. The desk and chair have already been moved out of the office for the meeting. Rebecca takes a chair to a most unbending individual who stares, straight ahead and keeps the arms folded. He is the only one who seems to abstain from the free-flowing drinks, the effect of which is already apparent on one or two.*

SHADRACH. No, Sister, we refuse to sit down. We refuse to sit down. We have been slighted and we make known our protest. We have been treated with less courtesy than becomes the leader of a denomination twenty thousand strong. Brother Jero, at whose behest we have presented ourselves here at great inconvenience, is not himself here to welcome us. We protest his discourtesy.

CALEB. Hear hear. (*Hiccups.*) Hardly the conduct of a gentleman prophet.

REBECCA. Brother Shadrach, I assure you he was held up by matters which concern this very affair you have come to discuss.

ISAAC. He is very long about it then.

SHADRACH. Much much too long, Sister Rebecca. To make us wait is an act of indignity thrust upon us.

ANANAIAS. Oh sit down, you fatuous old hypocrite.

SHADRACH *(turns to go)*. We take our leave.

CALEB. Hear hear. *(Hiccup.)* Let's all stage a dignified walk-out.

Nobody walks out these days. Not since the parliamentarians vanished.

ISAAC. Good old days those. Good for the profession.

CALEB. Come on, old Shad, give us a walk-out. *(With much difficulty on the word.)* An ecclesiastically dignified walkout.

REBECCA. Brother Shadrach, please …

SHADRACH. No, we take our leave. For the third time tonight we have been insulted by a common riff-raff of the calling. We take our leave.

CALEB. Hear hear. The honourable member for …

REBECCA. Pay no attention Brother. I apologize on their behalf.

Forgive us all for being remiss.

SHADRACH. I forgive you, Sister. *(Sits down.)*

ANANAIAS *(leans over the back of his chair)*. You will burst, Shadrach, you will burst like the frog in the swamp.

CALEB. Like the frog in the adage, Brother. *(Hiccup.)* Frog in the adage.

SHADRACH *(without losing his poise, whips his hand round and seizes that of ANANAIAS by the wrist and brings it round front. The hand is seen to contain a purse)*. Mine, I believe, Ananaias?

ANANAIAS. It dropped on the ground. Is that the thanks I get for helping you pick it up.

SHADRACH. I accuse no one, Ananaias. *(Returning wallet into the recesses of his robes.)* We are all met, I hope, in a spirit of brotherhood. The lesson reads, I am my brother's keeper Ananaias, not, I am my brother's pursekeeper.

ANANAIAS *(turns away)*. Lay not your treasures upon earth says the good book. Verily verily I say unto you, it is easier for a camel and so on and so forth.

CALEB *(raising his mug)*. Sister Rebecca, my spirits are low.

REBECCA *(rushing to fill it)*. Forgive me, Brother Caleb.

CALEB. Upliftment is in order, God bless you.

ISAAC. So where is this Jeroboam fellow? When is he coming to tell us why he has made us forsake our stations to wait on his lordship?

REBECCA. In a moment, Brother Matthew. *(Going to fill his mug.)*

ISAAC. I am not Brother Matthew …

REBECCA. I beg your pardon, Brother.

CALEB. A clear case of mistaken identity, Sister Rebecca.

ISAAC. I am not Brother Matthew, sister, and I beg you to note that fact.

MATTHEW *(nettled)*. May one ask just what you have against being Brother Matthew?

ISAAC. I know all about Brother Matthew, and that should be enough answer for anyone with a sense of shame.

REBECCA. Forgive my unfortunate error. Don't start a quarrel on that account.

ISAAC. And to think he has the nerve to show his face here. Some people are utterly without shame.

CALEB. Hear hear.

MATTHEW. And others are poor imitation Pharisees.

CALEB. Hear hear.

ISAAC. Better an imitation Pharisee than a sex maniac.

MATTHEW. I take exception to that!

ISAAC. Very good. Take exception.

MATTHEW. Dare repeat that and see if it doesn't land you in court for slander. Go on, we are all listening. I have witnesses. Come on I dare you.

ISAAC. I don't have to. We all know the truth. You may have been acquitted but we know the truth.

MATTHEW. Coward!

ISAAC. Fornicator.

MATTHEW. Drunkard, con-man. Forger.

CALEB. Three to one. Foul play.

REBECCA *(getting between them as they head for a dash).* Brothers, in the name of our common calling I beg of you …

JERO *and* CHUME *enter.* REBECCA *sighs with relief.*

Oh, Brother Jero, you are truly an answer to prayer.

JERO. Welcome, Brothers, welcome all of you and forgive me for arriving late at my own meeting. *(Hands* REBECCA *a key.)* Unlock the safe and bring out our secret weapon, Sister.

ISAAC. We have waited two hours, Brother.

ANANAIAS. You have not been here a half-hour Isaac. I saw you come in.

JERO. A-ah, I see empty mugs. No wonder our brothers are offended. Sister Rebecca, we require better hospitality.

REBECCA *(emerging with the file).* Do you think that wise, Brother Jero? They are already quite …

JERO. Trust me, I know what I am doing Sister. *(Loudly.)* More drinks for our brothers. Fill up the cups Sister Rebecca.

SHADRACH. We do not drink. We came here for a serious discussion, so we were informed. We have not come here to wine and dine.

JERO. We will not quarrel I admit the fault is mine. Sister Rebecca, some snuff for Brother Shadrach.

REBECCA. I shall get it at once, Brother Jero.

JERO *(turns and beams on the gathering).* And now, dear brother shepherds of the flock, let us waste no more time. We are mostly known to one another so I shall not waste your time on introductions. The subject is progress. Progress has caught up with us. Like the oceantide it is battering on our shore-line, the door-step of our tabernacle. Projects everywhere! Fun fairs! Gambling! Casinos! The servants of Mammon have had their heads turned by those foreign fleshpots to which they are drawn whenever they travel on their so-called economic missions. And our mission, the mission of the good Lord Jehovah shall be the sacrificial lamb, on the altar of Mammon.

Oh when you see smoke rising on that grievous day, know that it rises from these shacks of devotion which we have raised to shelter the son of God on his Visitation on that long-awaited day. And shall he find? What shall he find when he comes over the water, that great fisherman among men, thinking to step on to the open tabernacle which we, you and I, have founded here to await his glorious coming? *THIS! (With a flourish he pulls out a sheaf of photographs from his bag.)* This, my brothers!

JERO *observes their reactions as the photos of luscious scantily-clad bathers are circulated. Reactions vary from* SHADRACH *who turns away in calculated disgust to*

ANANAIAS *who finds them lewdly hilarious and* MATTHEW *who literally drools.*

SHADRACH. It must never happen here!

ISAAC. Never. We must organize.

CALEB. I concur. Rally the union. No business sharks in our spirituous waters.

ISAAC. All legitimate avenues of protest must be explored.

MATTHEW. What for?

ANANAIAS. What do you mean, what for?

MATTHEW. I said what for? These photos reveal strayed souls in need of salvation. Must we turn away from suchlike? Only the sick have need of the physician.

ISAAC. Not your kind of physic, Brother Matthew.

SHADRACH. If we take Brother Jeroboam's meaning correctly, and we think we do, the intention is to exclude … er … us, the physicians from this so-called resort is it not, Brother?

MATTHEW. We don't know that for certain.

JERO *(hands him the file at an open page).* Read this, Brother Matthew. These are the minutes of the meeting of Cabinet at which certain decisions were taken.

MATTHEW *(shrinks away).* What file is that?

JERO. Read it.

MATTHEW. It says Confidential on that paper. I don't want any government trouble.

ISAAC. Very wise of you, Brother Matthew. Mustn't risk your parole. *(Takes the file.)* I'll read it. *(At the first glance he whistles.)* How did you get hold of this, Jero?

JERO. The Lord moves in mysterious ways

ANANAIAS … His wonders to perform. Amen.

ISAAC *(reading).* 'Memorandum of the Cabinet Office to the Board of Tourism. Proposals to turn the Bar Beach into an a National Public Execution Amphitheatre.' Whew! You hadn't mentioned that.

JERO. I was saving it for a surprise. It is the heart of the whole business enterprise.

SHADRACH. We don't understand. Does this mean …?

JERO. Business, Brother Shadrach, big business.

MATTHEW. Where do we come in, in all this?

JERO. Patience, we're coming to it. Brother Isaac, do read on. Go down to the section titled Slum Clearance.

ISAAC *(his expression clouds in fury).* Hn? Hn? Hng !!!

MATTHEW. What is it? What is it?

ISAAC. Riff-raff! They call us riff-raff!

JERO. Read it out, Brother Isaac.

ISAAC. 'Unfortunately the beach is at present cluttered up with riff-raff of all sorts who dupe the citizenry and make the beach unattractive to decent and respectable people. Chiefest among these are the so-called …' Oh may the wrath of Jehovah smite them on their blasphemous mouths!

JERO *(taking back the file).* Time is short, Brothers. We cannot afford to be over-sensitive. *(Reads.)* '…the so-called prophets and evangelists. All these are not only to be immediately expelled but steps must be taken to ensure that they never at any time find their way back to the execution stadium.'

SHADRACH. Fire and brimstone! Sodom and Gomorrah!

JERO. Patience Brothers, patience. 'It is proposed however, that since the purpose of public execution is for the moral edification and spiritual upliftment of the people, one respectable religious denomination be licensed to operate on the Bar Beach. Such a body will say prayers before and after each execution, and where appropriate will administer the last rites to the condemned. They will be provided a point of vantage where they will preach to the public on the evil of crime and the morals to be drawn from the miserable end of the felons. After which their brass band shall provide religious music.'

ISAAC. A brass band? That means …

JERO. Yes, the Salvation Army.

SHADRACH. Enough. We have heard all we need to know of the conspiracy against us. The question now is, what do we do to foil them?

JERO. Organize. Band together. Brother Matthew is right: the sick have need of healing. We must not desert the iniquitous in their greatest hour of need.

SHADRACH (*looking towards* CALEB, *then* ANANAIAS). We foresee problems in banding together with certain members of the calling.

JERO. All problems can be overcome. The stakes are high, Brother Shadrach.

SHADRACH. The price is also high.

ANANAIAS. Oh shut up, you fatuous hypocrite!

SHADRACH. Ananaias!

JERO. Peace, Brothers, peace. Ananaias, I shall require greater decorum from you.

ANANAIAS. You have it before you ask, Brother Jero. Anything you say.

MATTHEW. What does Jeroboam have in mind, exactly? You didn't call us together without some idea in your head.

JERO. Quite correct, Brother Matthew. I have outlined certain plans of action and have even begun to pursue them. The time is short, in fact, the moment is now upon us. The Bar Beach becomes the single execution arena, the sole amphitheatre of death in the entire nation. Where at the moment we have spectators in thousands, the proposed stadium will seat hundreds of thousands. We must acquire the spiritual monopoly of such a captive congregation.

CALEB. Hear, hear!

ISAAC (*impatiently*). Yes, but how?

JERO. We form ONE body. Acquire a new image. Let the actuality of power see itself reflected in that image, reflected and complemented. We shall prophesy with one voice, not as lone voices crying in the wilderness, but as the united oracle of the spiritual profession.

CALEB. Brother Jero, I hand it to you. I couldn't have phrased it better and I pride myself on being a bookish sort of fellow.

MATTHEW. What image then?

JERO. Such an image as will make our outward colours one with theirs.

CALEB. Show them up in their true colours you mean. (*He splutters with laughter until he is coughing helplessly, near-choking.*)

JERO. Brother Caleb, I think that remark was in very bad taste.

MATTHEW (*wildly*). And dangerous. Very dangerous. I refuse to remain one moment longer if such remarks are permitted. We are not here to look for trouble. I dissociate myself from that remark.

ISAAC. Still watching your parole, Brother Matthew?

CALEB *(leans over drunkenly).* Psst. Is it true the magistrate was a sideman in your church?

JERO. Brothers, Brothers, this is no time for our private little quarrels. We must not envy Brother Matthew his spiritual influence in er... certain fortunate quarters when we are on the threshold of bringing the highest and the mightiest under our spiritual guidance.

SHADRACH. Are you day-dreaming? In a day or two you will not even have a roof over your head and you speak of ...

JERO. Yes Brother Shad, the highest and mightiest, I assure you, will come under our spiritual guidance.

SHADRACH. Success has swelled your head, Brother Jero.

CALEB. That's why he thinks big. *(Roars off alone into laughter.)*

JERO. Suppose I tell you, Shadrach, that it has come to the ears of the rulers that a certain new-formed religious body has prophesied a long life to the regime? That this mysterious body has declared that the Lord is so pleased with their er ... spectacular efforts to stamp out armed robbery, with the speed of the trials, the refusal of the right to appeal, the rejection of silly legal technicalities and the high rate of executions, that all these things are so pleasing to the Lord that he has granted eternal life to their regime?

SHADRACH. They won't believe you.

JERO. They have already. The seed was well planted and it has taken root. Tomorrow the Tourist Board shall propose a certain religious body for the new amphitheatre. The Cabinet will be informed that it is the same body which has made the prophecy. Our spiritual monopoly shall be approved without debate — Does anyone doubt me?

SHADRACH. The Shadrach-Medrach-Abednego Apostolic Trinity has a twenty-thousand strong congregation all over the country.

These include men from all walks of life including very high ranks within the uniformed profession. We propose therefore that our Apostolic Trinity absorb all other denominations into its spiritual bosom ...

The proposal is greeted with instant howls of rejection.

JERO. No, Brother Shadrach. As you see, it just will not do. Are there any other proposals?

They all shrug at one another.

ISAAC. All right Jero, let's have your proposal.

JERO. You all know Brother Chume. Prophet Chume I ought to say.

MATTHEW. But he's the one who went off his head.

ANANAIAS. Looks saner than you or me. Cleaner anyway.

JERO. Prophet Chume has left the ranks of the enemy and cast his lot among us. With his help, with the intimate knowledge which he has acquired of the workings of that foreign body to which he once belonged we shall recreate ourselves in the required image. We shall manifest our united spiritual essence in the very form and shape of the rulers of the land. Nothing, you will agree could be more respectable than that. *(Rises.)* Sister Rebecca, bring out the banner!

REBECCA *(runs out with the flag, flushed with excitement).* Is this the moment, Brother Jero?

JERO. The moment is now, Sister. Witness now the birth of the first Church of the Apostolic Salvation Army of the Lord!

CHUME *begins the tune of* 'Are you washed in the Blood of the Lamb'.

REBECCA *sings lustily, deaf to the world.*

Behold the new body of the Lord! Forward into battle, Brothers!

ISAAC. Against what?

JERO. Precisely.

SHADRACH *(disdainfully).* Precisely what? He asks, against what? You say, precisely.

JERO. Precisely. Against what? We don't know any more than our secular models. They await a mirade, we will provide it.

SHADRACH *(indicating* CHUME). With lunatics like him. You fancy yourself an empire-builder.

JERO. A spiritual empire builder, Brother Shadrach. Those who are not with us, are against us. This is the Salvation Army with a difference. With pepper and ogiri. With ngwam-ngwan. Right, Brother Chume?

CHUME *nods vigorously without stopping the music.*

ISAAC. Hey, you haven't said who is to be head of this Army.

CALEB. Good point. Very good point.

JERO. We come in as equals. We form a syndicate.

SHADRACH. Everybody needs a head.

CALEB *(solemnly).* Old Shad is de-ee-eep. *(Hiccups.)*

JERO. A titular head. He gives the orders and keeps close watch on the church treasury. Purely ceremonial.

ISAAC. Yes, but who? Who do you have in mind for Captain?

JERO. Captain, Brother Isaac? No, no, not captain. We must not cut our image small in the eyes of the world. General, at least.

SHADRACH. And who would that be, you still haven't said.

JERO. Whoever has the secrets of the Tourist Board in his hands.

Whoever can guarantee that the new body does obtain nomination from the Tourist Board.

ANANAIAS. I knew it. I knew he was keeping something to himself.

ISAAC. You have thought of everything, haven't you?

JERO. You may say I am divinely inspired, Brother Isaac.

SHADRACH. And you, we presume, are in possession of the aforesaid secrets?

JERO. Have we a united body or not?

ANANAIAS. Christ! Those fat pockets begging to be picked while their owners are laughing at the poor devil at the stake. It's a sin to be missing from this garden of Eden. *(Throws* JERO *a salute.)* General! Reporting for duty, sir.

JERO *(saluting in turn).* Sergeant-major! Go in the room and find a uniform that fits you.

ISAAC. Millionaire businessmen! Expensive sinners coming to enjoy the Bar Beach show.

JERO. Who else is for the Army of the Lord?

ISAAC. It's Sodom and Gomorrah. The milk is sour and the honey is foul.

JERO. Who is for the Army of the Lord?

ISAAC. What rank do you have in mind for me?

JERO. Major. *(Gestures.)* In there. You'll find a uniform that fits you.

As he goes in ANANAIAS *returns singing lustily and banging a tambourine. He is uniformed in what looks like a Salvation Army outfit except for the cap which is the 'indigenous' touch, made in local material and 'abetiaja' style. The combination is ludicrous.*

MATTHEW (*takes another look at the picture of a curvaceous bathing belle and decides*). I used to play the flute a little, Brother Jer… I mean General Jeroboam. In fact I was once in my school band.

JERO. You'll find a uniform in there, Captain.

SHADRACH. The uniform will not change you. You will still be the same Bar Beach riff-raff no matter what you wear. Nobody will give you a monopoly.

CALEB. Wrong on all counts, Brother Shad. By the cut of his tailor shall a man be known. Uniform maketh man.

JERO. Very soon the syndicate will be dosed. The Army hierarchy is for foundation members only. We hold office by divine grace, in perpetuity. Join now or quit.

SHADRACH. Overreacher. We know your kind, Jeroboam. Continue to count your chickens.

CALEB. Wrong again, Shad. You don't know the worthy Jero it seems. If he says he'll get the monopoly, he will. A thorough methodical man, very much after my heart.

JERO. What rank do you want, Caleb?

CALEB. I'll stick out for Colonel. I may be slightly (*Hiccups.*) see what I mean, but I know what's what. I'm an educated man and that's a rare commodity in this outfit. Present company naturally excepted, General.

JERO. Lieutenant-Colonel.

CALEB. General, I'm thinking that instead of merely preaching at the assembly we could do a morality play, you know, something like our Easter and Christmas Cantata. I'm quite nifty at things like that — The Rewards of Sin, The Terrible End of the Desperado … and so on. Well er … that sort of specialized duties deserves a higher rank don't you think, mon General?

JERO (*firmly*). Lieutenant-Colonel.

CALEB (*throws a drunken salute*). So be it, mon General.

Goes in. The others are coming out, uniformed.

JERO. You are alone, Shadrach.

SHADRACH. We are never alone. We proceed this minute to the Chairman of the Tourist Board, there to put an end to our ambitions. The much-respected aunt of the Chairman is a devout member of our flock.

JERO (*looks at his watch*). If you wish to see the Chief Executive Officer in person he will arrive in a few minutes. He was invited to this meeting.

SHADRACH. Here?

JERO. He will negotiate for the other side.

SHADRACH. Bluff! The only officer you'll see here is the Eviction Officer.

ANANAIAS (*looking out*). My General, the enemy is without!

JERO. Let him pass freely.

ANANAIAS. What do they want? (*Going to the door.*) You're back are you? Lucky for you the General gives you safe conduct.

EXECUTIVE. You have a nerve summoning us here at this time of night. (*Blocking his ears.*) Will you tell them to stop that lunatic din!

JERO. Colonel Chume …

ANANALAS. He won't hear. I'll stop him for you.

Goes over, salutes and takes the trumpet from his mouth.

JERO. Sit down.

EXECUTIVE. I demand …

JERO. Seat him down Sergeant-Major.

ANANAIAS. My pleasure, General, sir.

Forces down the CHIEF EXECUTIVE *into a chair. The* CLERK *quickly scurries into a seat.*

JERO. Excuse me while I get ready for the negotiations.

He picks the file off the table with deliberate movements. The EXECUTIVE OFFICER *stares at the file fascinated. He exchanges looks with the* CLERK *who quickly looks down.* JERO *goes into the room.*

SHADRACH. We are, we presume, in the presence of the Chief Eviction Officer of the Tourist Board.

CLERK. No, that's C.E.O. II. This is C.E.O. I, Chief Executive Officer. C.E.O. III is still to be appointed – that's the Chief Execution Officer, a new post.

EXECUTIVE *(turns to inspect* SHADRACH *slowly, like a strange insect).* And who might you be?

SHADRACH. Leader of the Shadrach-Medrach-Abednego Apostolic flock, twenty thousand strong.

EXECUTIVE *(wearily).* Another fanatic.

SHADRACH. It is our hope that you have come here to put an end to the schemes of this rapacious trader on piety who calls himself …

EXECUTIVE. Oh Christ!

Enter JERO, *resplendent in a Salvation Army General uniform.* CHUME *blares a fanfare on the trumpet.*

JERO. The file, Sister Rebecca.

EXECUTIVE. And now I hope you will …

JERO. You came, I trust, alone as requested.

EXECUTIVE. Yes I foolishly risked my life coming without protection to this haunt of cut-throats.

JERO. It was entirely in your own interests.

EXECUTIVE. So you said. And now perhaps you will kindly tell me what my interests are.

JERO. They are such as might be unsuitable for the ears of a policeman. That is why I suggested that you leave your escort behind.

EXECUTIVE. Come to the point.

JERO *(takes a seat, carefully brushing his creases).* You will remember that when the Chief Eviction Officer was compelled, as a result of the violent spiritual conversion of Colonel Rebecca …

EXECUTIVE. Colonel who?

JERO. Colonel Rebecca of the Church of the Apostolic Salvation Army. CASA for short. Do you know that Casa means home? In this case, spiritual home. I am sure you approve our new image.

Enter REBECCA *with file. She is now in uniform.*

EXECUTIVE. Your image does not interest me in the slightest.

JERO. And your own image Chief Executive Officer?

Hands him two sheets of paper from the file.

Great is the Lord and Mighty in his ways. He led your Chief Eviction Officer to my door in the company of one He had marked down for salvation, overwhelmed him with the onslaught of such hot holiness that he fled leaving his documents in the possession of a woman possessed.

EXECUTIVE. What do you want? Just say what you want?

JERO. Monopoly is the subject of your file No. I.B.P. stroke 537 stroke 72A. Beauty parlours, supermarkets, restaurants, cafés and ice-cream kiosks, fair-grounds, construction and hiring of beach huts, amusement gadgets, gambling machines and dodgems and roundabouts and parking facilities — for the new National Amphitheatre to be built on the Bar Beach. Mr Executive Officer, the list is endless, but what is of interest to the good Lord whose interests I represent is the method of awarding these very superabundant contracts.

EXECUTIVE. No need to talk so loud. *(Looks round nervously.)* Just say what you want.

JERO. Render unto Caesar what is Caesar's, and unto God what is God's.

EXECUTIVE. What does that mean in plain Caesar's language?

JERO. A monopoly on spirituality.

EXECUTIVE. What's that?

JERO. Made out to the Church of the Apostolic Salvation Army. CASA.

SHADRACH. We on this side place our trust in your integrity not to accede to any such request.

EXECUTIVE. Will someone tell me who this fellow is?

JERO. Colonel Rebecca has been kind enough to prepare the letter. It requires only your signature she tells me.

EXECUTIVE *(taking the letter, incredulous).* Is that all? Just a monopoly on the rights to hold religious rallies here?

JERO. It's enough.

EXECUTIVE. Not even a monopoly on some small business enterprise?

JERO. We are already in business. Of course we expect you to declare that all land actually occupied as of now by the various religious bodies would from now on be held in trust, managed and developed by the newly approved representative body of all apostolic bodies, CASA …

EXECUTIVE. What!

SHADRACH. Mr Executive Officer …

EXECUTIVE. What has that to do with monopoly on spirituality?

JERO. Spirituality, to take root, must have land to take root in.

EXECUTIVE. Yes, yes, of course, I — er — see your point.

JERO. Our image also conforms on all levels. We are not fanatics. Our symbol is blood. It washes all sins away. *All* sins, Mr Tourist Board.

EXECUTIVE. Yes, indeed. A point decidedly in your favour.

SHADRACH. We protest, sir. We strongly protest!

EXECUTIVE. Who is this man?

JERO. An apostate. Ignore him. (SHADRACH *splutters speechlessly.* JERO *pushes a piece of paper to the official.)* The declaration. It says nothing but the truth. You are present at the meeting for apostolic union. You see yourself the new body which has emerged, fully representative.

SHADRACH. Thieves! Robbers! Rapists and cut-throats!

JERO. We did not include you, Brother Shadrach.

The EXECUTIVE OFFICER *signs, then* JERO *pushes it to the* CLERK.

Witness it. *(The* CLERK *looks at* EXECUTIVE OFFICER.)

EXECUTIVE. Sign the damn thing and let's get out of here.

JERO *(hands the paper to* REBECCA). Are those their genuine signatures, Colonel?

EXECUTIVE *(offended)*. I don't double-deal. I am a man of my word.

JERO. It isn't that I don't trust you.

REBECCA. It is their signatures, my General.

EXECUTIVE. And now may I have …

JERO. Your list of contracts? Just one more paper to be signed. The attachment. The survey map which indicates what portions of the beach are referred to as trust property of CASA.

EXECUTIVE. This is impossible. We have allocated some of the land squatted on by your —

JERO. Please give me the credit of having done my home-work. You forget we have had a formidable ally in the person of Colonel Rebecca, your former Confidential Secretary. And we have drawn on that precious file which your Eviction Officer so generously loaned us. There is no duplication, check it if you wish.

EXECUTIVE. All right, all right. *(About to sign.)*

SHADRACH. Don't sign your soul away to the devil, sir!

EXECUTIVE. Can't you shut him up?

JERO. Sergeant-major!

ANANAIAS. My pleasure sir. Come on, Shad.

Holds him expertly by the elbow and ejects him.

SHADRACH. We protest most strenuously at this barefaced conspiracy. We shall pursue it to the highest level. The leader of a flock twenty thousand strong is not to be taken lightly we promise you

EXECUTIVE. Are you sure he won't make trouble later? *(He signs.)*

JERO. Leave him to us. The testimony of the Salvation Army will weigh against that of a disgruntled charlatan anywhere. *(Takes the map and returns the incriminating papers.)* Your documents, sir. I hope you take better care of them next time.

EXECUTIVE *(grabs them quickly, glances through and stuffs them in his pockets)*. And now to go and deal with that stupid Eviction Officer.

JERO. Blame him not. The power of the spirit on murky souls overcomes the strictest civil service discipline.

EXECUTIVE. Don't preach at me, humbug.

JERO. On the contrary we will preach at you. Every Tuesday at twelve o'clock the Church of Apostolic Salvation Army will preach outside your office. The subject of our sermons shall be, the evils of corruption — of the soul. We intend to restrict ourselves to spiritual matters. We will not contradict the secular image.

The CLERK bursts our laughing. The EXECUTIVE eyes him balefully and the laughter dries on his face.

EXECUTIVE. You report to me in my office first thing tomorrow morning. You and the Eviction Officer. *(Storms out.)*

ANANAIAS *(as the* CHIEF CLERK *hesitates)*. Hey you, follow your master.

CLERK. Er … Brother … I mean … er — General, you wouldn't … I mean … by any chance … what I mean to say is … even a Lance-Corporal would do me.

REBECCA. Glory be! *(Rushes forward to embrace him.)* I think there is a uniform just his size, my General.

JERO. As you wish Colonel, Lance-Corporal it is then.

ANANAIAS. What next, my General?

JERO. No time like the present. We march this moment and show the flag. Brother Chume, kneel for your second christening. Or third. I'm beginning to lose count. (CHUME *kneels.* JERO *anoints his head.*) Go down, Brother Chume, rise Brigadier Joshua!

SEVERALLY *(amidst embraces).* God bless you, Joshua. God bless Brigadier Joshua.

CHUME *(overwhelmed).* Oh Brother — sorry General — Jero. I am so unworthy …

JERO. Nonsense, Churne, you are the very ornament of your rank. Stand to action Brigade. Brigadier Joshua will lead, blowing the trumpet. Sergeant Ananaias!

ANANAIAS. My General?

JERO. When Joshua blows the trumpet, it will be your duty to make the miracle happen. The walls shall come tumbling down or you will have some explaining to do.

ANANAIAS. Leave it to me, my General.

JERO. Just lean on the rotting walls Ananaias and the Lord will do the rest. By dawn the entire beach must be cleansed of all pestilential separatist shacks which infest the holy atmosphere of the united apostolate of the Lord. Beginning naturally with Apostate Shadrach's unholy den. The fire and the sword, Ananaias, the fire and the sword. Light up the night of evil with the flames of holiness! Consecrate the grounds for the Bar Beach Spectacular!

ANANAIAS. Apostolic Army of the Lord, Atten… tion! Forward, Banner of the Lord! (REBECCA *takes up position.*) Forward, Trumpet of the Lord! (CHUME *positions himself.*) Sound the Trumpet! By the left, Quick … Swing against Corruption!

CHUME *blasts the first bar of 'Joshua Fit the Battle of Jericho' in strict tempo, then swings elated into a brisk indigenous rhythm to which the Army march–dance out into the right.*

JERO, *with maximum condescension acknowledges the salute of the army. As the last man disappears, he takes a last look at the framed photo, takes it down and places it face towards the wall, takes from a drawer in the table an even larger photo of himself in his present uniform and mounts it on the wall. He then seats himself at the table and pulls towards him a file or two, as if to start work. Looks up suddenly and on his face is the amiable-charlatan.*

JERO. After all, it is the fashion these days to be a desk General.

Blackout.

Understanding action and structure

Jero's Metamorphosis is a political satire. According to Doctor Johnson, a famous eighteenth-century critic, satire is writing 'in which wickedness or folly is censured'. In this play it is the everyday corruption of the military government that is being held up to ridicule. Jero is a religious fraud, or charlatan, who intends to make as much money and gain as much power as he can through his 'religious' activities.

The play is a short piece, delivered in three scenes. In the first scene Jero is organising a meeting of all the beach prophets to respond to the changing circumstances at Bar Beach. He has been helped in his plans by Sister Rebecca, a former government employee who has brought Jero a sensitive government file. At the end of the scene, Sister Rebecca obtains more information from government executives who have come to reclaim the earlier file.

Wole Soyinka has written many plays about the political problems of his country and has used his writing to challenge the government. He was imprisoned for a time for his beliefs.

The second scene is a broadly comic episode where Chume, a member of the Salvation Army, is rehearsing his trumpet playing in front of Major Da Silva, a Salvation Army officer. However they end up in argument and Da Silva escapes. Jero enters and convinces Chume to join his organisation.

The third scene (the extract in this book) shows how Jero manages to take advantage of the situation and outflank his enemies.

- Why do you think that the drinks are 'free flowing' at the beginning of this scene?
- Who is the main opponent of Jero's plans amongst the preachers at the meeting?

Look at the text on pages 125–6 from:

'JERO. Excuse me while I get ready for the negotiations.'

down to

'SHADRACH. Thieves! Robbers! Rapists and cut-throats!

JERO. We did not include you, Brother Shadrach'

- How does Jero get his way in this episode?
- What is the Executive's response?
- What is Shadrach's reaction?

Understanding character

Jero has been seen in an earlier Soyinka play, *The Trials of Brother Jero*, where his character, the rogue religious leader, was first established. He has since moved up a little in the world and is adapting to the world of military rule, but he is still the trickster and schemer of the earlier play.

Read the text on page 122 from:

'ISAAC. All right, Jero, let's have your proposal.'

down to

'JERO. Captain, Brother Isaac? No, no, not captain. We must not cut our image small in the eyes of the world. General, at least.'

- How does Jero use the situation here to gain an advantage?
- What is the importance of Chume to this arrangement?
- Why does he think the organisation should have a General?

The third scene also contains a number of minor characters that are very entertaining in themselves.

- How does Soyinka present Shadrach, Matthew and The Executive?

Understanding themes

Satirical writing is intended to serve as a warning. Read the following passage:

> JERO. Suppose I tell you, Shadrach, that it has come to the ears of the rulers that a certain new-formed religious body has prophesied a long life to the regime? That this mysterious body has declared that the Lord is so pleased with their er... spectacular efforts to stamp out our armed robbery, with the speed of the trials, the refusal of the right to appeal, the rejection of silly legal technicalities and the high rate of executions, that all these things are so pleasing to the Lord that he has granted eternal life to their regime?

- What features of the government's actions is Jero praising?
- Do you think the audience is meant to support Jero here?
- Why do you think Soyinka has included this kind of material?

Understanding dramatic devices

Irony

The main dramatic device that Soyinka uses is irony. We see an unscrupulous opportunist trying to make as much as he can from a very unpleasant situation. We hear about plans and schemes which Jero thinks are wonderful. We hear about the ways that Jero and others would benefit from public executions.

Now, all of these aspects are meant to disturb and amuse an audience. We are meant to be shocked rather than pleased with Jero's plans. Therefore the writer has a different meaning from what is presented to us on the surface level of words and actions. This difference between what is written and what is meant produces irony.

Allegory

Another device that is used is allegory. This is where the events on stage are meant to represent events in real life. A very good example is when Jero is allocating ranks in his new Church of the Apostolic Salvation Army. This is meant to indicate the way in which officers and politicians get their positions under the military government.

Understanding performance

Farce

Jero's Metamorphosis has a number of features of farce, the kind of drama which produces laughter through highly improbable events. Examples of farce are the opening, with the prophets drinking freely, Ananaias's attempted theft of Shadrach's wallet, Chume's trumpet playing, Rebecca's singing and the military mockery, e.g. where Ananaias salutes Jero and it is returned.

Tasks

Personal response: writing

1   What features of *Jero's Metamorphosis* make it interesting theatre?

You should write about:
a) events
b) characters
c) ideas
d) humour, farce and irony.

Practical activities

Individually or in pairs

2   Choose three recent political issues that could benefit from some kind of dramatisation and draw up ideas for plays based on each. These should not be lengthy proposals, but more like a 'pitch', the kind of simple idea that is used in the film industry to gain finance.

3   Pick on three occupations in modern Britain that have some similarities with Jero's 'preacher' and give your reasons why you have selected them.

4   Research Soyinka's Nobel Prize by accessing:

http://www.nobel.se/laureates/literature-1986-1-bio.html

In groups

5   Allocate parts and act out the scene.

Useful notes

prophets	leaders of religious cults
slighted	offended, a word typical of Shadrach's rather stuffy English
parliamentarians	politicians (who are no longer present under military rule)
fatuous	foolish or silly
adage	proverb
lay not…camel	Biblical references which question the importance of wealth to an individual
stations	places on the beach where the prophets 'preach'
servants of Mammon	business people (Mammon being the devil of covetousness)
parole	being let out of prison on a word of honour
Bar Beach	a beach in Lagos
Public Execution Amphitheatre	where public executions took place, under military rule
felons	criminals guilty of felony (a major crime)
Shadrach-Meshnach-Abednego	three young men, in the Bible, whose faith kept them alive despite being put into a fiery furnace
ogiri, ngwam-ngwam	Nigerian foods, but the point being made is that the new organisation will be a Nigerian Salvation Army

Classic Irish Drama: *The Plough and the Stars* by Sean O'Casey

Background and context

Sean O'Casey was born in Dublin in 1880 and grew up facing poverty after his father's death. As a young man he was active in politics but rejected it in favour of the theatre.

O'Casey's reputation rests mainly on three great plays: *Juno and the Paycock, The Shadow of a Gunman* and *The Plough and the Stars*. Each of these plays is set in the period of the Irish 'Troubles' of the early part of the twentieth century and uses as a backdrop the Dublin slum life that O'Casey knew from his own experience. They all mix tragedy and comedy and for that reason are often called 'tragicomedies'.

The Plough and the Stars is considered to be the most ambitious of the three great plays and rightly so. It depicts with honesty and conviction the way a number of people responded to the turmoil of the Easter Rebellion of 1916. O'Casey did not present a particularly patriotic position in this play and when it was first put on at the Abbey Theatre in Dublin in 1924, it provoked riots. Critics said that the play insulted the Irish people, but the poet W. B. Yeats came to O'Casey's defence when he spoke out against the critics. However, O'Casey was wounded by the criticism and by the later rejection of *The Silver Tassie* and so he left Ireland to live in England where he remained until his death in 1964.

The Plough and the Stars

Act 3

The events in the following extract occur in and around the Clitheroe household (home of Nora and Jack Clitheroe).

A fashionably dressed, middle-aged, stout woman comes hurriedly in, and makes for the group. She is almost fainting with fear.

WOMAN: For Gawd's sake, will one of you kind men show any safe way for me to get to Wrathmines? ... I was foolish enough to visit a friend, thinking the howl thing was a joke, and now I cawn't get a car or a tram to take me home — isn't it awful?
FLUTHER: I'm afraid, ma'am, one way is as safe as another.
WOMAN: And what am I gowing to do? Oh, isn't this awful? ... I'm so different from others ... The mowment I hear a shot, my legs give way under me — I cawn't stir, I'm paralysed — isn't it awful?
FLUTHER: *(moving away)* It's a derogatory way to be, right enough, ma'am.

WOMAN: *(catching Fluther's coat)* Creeping along the street there, with my head down and my eyes half shut, a bullet whizzed past within an inch of my nowse … I had to lean against the wall for a long time, gasping for breath — I nearly passed away — it was awful! … I wonder, would you kind men come some of the way and see me safe?

FLUTHER: I have to go away, ma'am, to thry an' save a few things from th' burnin' buildin's.

THE COVEY: Come on, then, or there won't be anything left to save.

The Covey and Fluther hurry away.

WOMAN: *(to Peter)* Wasn't it an awful thing for me to leave my friend's house? Wasn't it an idiotic thing to do? … I haven't the slightest idea where I am … You have a kind face, sir. Could you possibly come and pilot me in the direction of Wrathmines?

PETER: *(indignantly)* D'ye think I'm goin' to risk me life throttin' in front of you? An' maybe get a bullet that would gimme a game leg or something that would leave me a jibe an' a jeer to Fluther an' th' young Covey for th' rest o' me days! *(With an indignant toss of his head he walks into the house.)*

WOMAN: *(going out)* I know I'll fall down in a dead faint if I hear another shot go off anyway near me — isn't it awful!

Bessie Burgess, played by Dame Judi Dench at the Young Vic in 1991.

Mrs Gogan comes out of the house pushing a pram before her. As she enters the street, Bessie rushes out, follows Mrs Gogan, and catches hold of the pram, stopping Mrs Gogan's progress.

BESSIE: Here, where are you goin' with that? How quick you were, me lady, to clap your eyes on th' pram … Maybe you don't know that Mrs Sullivan, before she went to spend Easther with her people in Dunboyne, gave me sthrict injunctions to give an accasional look to see if it was still standin' where it was left in th' corner of th' lobby.

MRS GOGAN: That remark of yours, Mrs Bessie Burgess, requires a little considheration, seein' that th' pram was left on our lobby, an' not on yours; a foot or two a little to th' left of th' jamb of me own room door; nor is it needful to mention th' name of th' person that gave a squint to see if it was there th' first thing in th' mornin', an' th' last thing in th' stillness o' th' night; never failin' to realize that her eyes couldn't be goin' wrong, be sthretchin' out her arm an' runnin' her hand over th' pram, to make sure that th' sight was no deception! Moreover, somethin's tellin' me that th' runnin' hurry of an inthrest you're takin' in it now is a sudden ambition to use th' pram for a purpose that a loyal woman of law an' ordher would stagger away from! *(She gives the pram a sudden push that pulls Bessie forward.)*

BESSIE: *(still holding the pram)* There's not as much as one body in th' house that doesn't know that it wasn't Bessie Burgess that was always shakin' her voice complainin' about people leavin' bassinettes in th' way of them that, week in an' week out, had to pay their rent, an' always had to find a regular accommodation for her own furniture in her own room … An' as for law an' ordher, puttin' aside th' harp an' shamrock, Bessie Burgess 'll have as much respect as she wants for th' lion an' unicorn!

PETER: *(appearing at the door)* I think I'll go with th' pair of yous an' see th' fun. A fella might as well chance it, anyhow.

MRS GOGAN: *(taking no notice of Peter, and pushing the pram on another step)* Take your rovin' lumps o' hands from pattin' th' bassinette, if you please, ma'am; an', steppin' from th' threshold of good manners, let me tell you, Mrs Burgess, that's it's a fat wondher to Jennie Gogan that a lady-like singer o' hymns like yourself would lower her thoughts from sky-thinkin' to sthretch out her arm in a sly-seekin' way to pinch anything dhriven asthray in th' confusion of th' battle our boys is makin' for th' freedom of their counthry!

PETER: *(laughing and rubbing his hands together)* Hee, hee, hee, hee, hee! I'll go with th' pair o' yous an' give yous a hand.

MRS GOGAN: *(with a rapid turn of her head as she shoves the pram forward)* Get up in th' prambulator an' we'll wheel you down.

BESSIE: *(to Mrs Gogan)* Poverty an' hardship has sent Bessie Burgess to abide with sthrange company, but she always knew them she had to live with from backside to breakfast time; an' she can tell them, always havin' had a Christian kinch on her conscience, that a passion for thievin' an' pinchin' would find her soul a foreign place to live in, an' that her present intention is quite th' lofty-hearted one of pickin' up anything shaken up an' scatthered about in th' loose confusion of a general plundher!

By this time they have disappeared from view. Peter is following, when the boom of a big gun in the distance brings him to a quick halt.

PETER: God Almighty, that's th' big gun again! God forbid any harm would happen to them, but sorra mind I'd mind if they met with a dhrop in their mad endeyvours to plundher an' desthroy.

He looks down the street for a moment, then runs to the hall door of the house, which is open, and shuts it with a vicious pull; he then goes to the chair in which Mollser had sat, sits down, takes out his pipe, lights it and begins to smoke with his head carried at a haughty angle. The Covey comes staggering in with a ten-stone sack of flour on his back. On the top of the sack is a ham. He goes over to the door, pushes it with his head, and finds he can't open it; he turns slightly in the direction of Peter.

THE COVEY: *(to Peter)* Who shut th' door?… *(He kicks at it.)* Here, come on an' open it, will you? This isn't a hand-bag I've got on me back.

PETER: Now, me young Covey, d'ye think I'm goin' to be your lackey?

THE COVEY: *(angrily)* Will you open th' door, y'oul' —

PETER: *(shouting)* Don't be assin' me to open any door, don't be assin' me to open any door for you … Makin' a shame an' a sin o' th' cause that good men are fightin' for … Oh, God forgive th' people that, instead o' burnishin' th' work th' boys is doin' today with quiet honesty an' patience, is revilin' their sacrifices with a riot of lootin' an' roguery!

THE COVEY: Isn't your own eyes leppin' out o' your head with envy that you haven't th' guts to ketch a few o' th' things that God is givin' to His chosen people? … Y'oul' hypocrite, if everyone was blind you'd steal a cross off an ass's back!

PETER: *(very calmly)* You're not going to make me lose me temper; you can go on with your proddin' as long as you like; goad an' goad an' goad away; hee, hee, heee! I'll not lose me temper.

Somebody opens door and the Covey goes in.

THE COVEY: *(inside, mockingly)* Cuckoo-oo!

PETER: *(running to the door and shouting in a blaze of passion as he follows the Covey in)* You lean, long, lanky lath of a lowsey bastard … *(Following him in)* Lowsey bastard, lowsey bastard!

Bessie and Mrs Gogan enter, the pride of a great joy illuminating their faces. Bessie is pushing the pram, which is filled with clothes and boots; on the top of the boots and clothes is a fancy table, which Mrs Gogan is holding on with her left hand, while with her right hand she holds a chair on the top of her head. They are heard talking to each other before they enter.

MRS GOGAN: *(outside)* I don't remember ever havin' seen such lovely pairs as them, *(they appear)* with'th' pointed toes an' th' cuban heels.

BESSIE: They'll go grand with th' dhresses we're afther liftin', when we've stitched a sthray bit o' silk to lift th' bodices up a little bit higher, so as to shake th' shame out o' them; an' make them fit for women that hasn't lost themselves in th' nakedness o' th' times.

They fussily carry in the chair, the table, and some of the other goods. They return to bring in the rest.

PETER: *(at door, sourly to Mrs Gogan)* Ay, you. Mollser looks as if she was goin' to faint, an' your youngster is roam' in convulsions in her lap.

MRS GOGAN: *(snappily)* She's never any other way but faintin'!

She goes to go in with some things in her arms, when a shot from a rifle rings out. She and Bessie make a bolt for the door, which Peter, in a panic, tries to shut before they have got inside.

Ay, ay, ay, you cowardly oul' fool, what are you thryin' to shut th' door on us for?

They retreat tumultuously inside. A pause; then Captain Brennan comes in supporting Lieutenant Langon, whose arm is around Brennan's neck. Langon's face, which is ghastly white, is momentarily convulsed with spasms of agony. He is in a state of collapse, and Brennan is almost carrying him. After a few moments Clitheroe, pale, and in a state of calm nervousness, follows, looking back in the direction from which he came, a rifle, held at the ready, in his hands.

CAPT. BRENNAN: *(savagely to Clitheroe)* Why did you fire over their heads? Why didn't you fire to kill?

CLITHEROE: No, no, Bill; bad as they are they're Irish men an' women.

CAPT. BRENNAN: *(savagely)* Irish be damned! Attackin' an' mobbin' th' men that are riskin' their lives for them. If these slum lice gather at our heels again, plug one o' them, or I'll soon shock them with a shot or two meself!

LIEUT. LANGON: *(moaningly)* My God, is there ne'er an ambulance knockin' around anywhere? … Th' stomach is ripped out o' me; I feel it — o-o-oh, Christ!

CAPT. BRENNAN: Keep th' heart up, Jim; we'll soon get help, now.

Nora rushes wildly out of the house and flings her arms round the neck of Clitheroe with a fierce and joyous insistence. Her hair is down, her face is haggard, but her eyes are agleam with the light of happy relief.

NORA: Jack, Jack, Jack; God be thanked … be thanked He has been kind and merciful to His poor handmaiden … My Jack, my own Jack, that I thought was lost is found, that I thought was dead is alive again!

Oh, God be praised for ever, evermore! … My poor Jack … Kiss me, kiss me, Jack, kiss your own Nora!

CLITHEROE: *(kissing her, and speaking brokenly)* My Nora; my little, beautiful Nora, I wish to God I'd never left you.

NORA: It doesn't matter — not now, not now, Jack. It will make us dearer than ever to each other … Kiss me, kiss me again.

CLITHEROE: Now, for God's sake, Nora, don't make a scene.

NORA: I won't, I won't; I promise, I promise, Jack; honest to God. I'll be silent an' brave to bear th' joy of feelin' you safe in my arms again … It's hard to force away th' tears of happiness at th' end of an awful agony.

BESSIE: *(from the upper window)* Th' Minsthrel Boys aren't feelin' very comfortable now. Th' big guns has knocked all th' harps out of their hands. General Clitheroe'd rather be unlacin' his wife's bodice than standin' at a barricade. An' th' professor of chicken-butcherin' there, finds he's up against somethin' a little tougher even than his own chickens, an' that's sayin' a lot!

CAPT. BRENNAN: *(up to Bessie)* Shut up, y'oul' hag!

BESSIE: *(down to Brennan)* Choke th' chicken, choke th' chicken, choke th' chicken!

LIEUT. LANGON: For God's sake, Bill, bring me some place where me wound 'll be looked afther … Am I to die before anything is done to save me?

CAPT. BRENNAN: *(to Clitheroe)* Come on, Jack. We've got to get help for Jim, here — have you no thought for his pain an' danger?

BESSIE: Choke th' chicken, choke th' chicken, choke th' chicken!

CLITHEROE: *(to Nora)* Loosen me, darling, let me go.

NORA: *(clinging to him)* No, no, no, I'll not let you go! Come on, come up to our home, Jack, my sweetheart, my lover, my husband, an' we'll forget th' last few terrible days! … I look tired now, but a few hours of happy rest in your arms will bring back th' bloom of freshness again, an' you will be glad, you will be glad, glad … glad!

LIEUT. LANGON: Oh, if I'd kep' down only a little longer, I mightn't ha' been hit! Everyone else escapin', an' me gettin' me belly ripped asundher! … I couldn't scream, couldn't even scream … D'ye think I'm really badly wounded, Bill? Me clothes seem to be all soakin' wet … It's blood … My God, it must be me own blood!

CAPT. BRENNAN: *(to Clitheroe)* Go on, Jack, bid her goodbye with another kiss, an' be done with it! D'ye want Langon to die in me arms while you're dallyin' with your Nora?

CLITHEROE: *(to Nora)* I must go, I must go, Nora. I'm sorry we met at all … It couldn't be helped — all other ways were blocked be th' British … Let me go, can't you, Nora? D'ye want me to be unthrue to me comrades?

NORA: No, I won't let you go … I want you to be thrue to me, Jack … I'm your dearest comrade; I'm your thruest comrade … They only want th' comfort of havin' you in th' same danger as themselves … Oh, Jack, I can't let you go!

CLITHEROE: You must, Nora, you must.

NORA: All last night at th' barricades I sought you, Jack. I didn't think of th' danger — I could only think of you … I asked for you everywhere … Some o' them laughed … I was pushed away, but I shoved back … Some o' them even sthruck me, … an' I screamed an' screamed your name!

Jack (Tony Doyle) and Nora (Susan Fleetwood) at the National Theatre, 1977.

CLITHEROE: *(in fear her action would give him future shame)* What possessed you to make a show of yourself, like that? What way d'ye think I'll feel when I'm told my wife was bawlin' for me at th' barricades? What are you more than any other woman?

NORA: No more, maybe; but you are more to me than any other man, Jack … I didn't mean any harm, honestly, Jack … I couldn't help it. … I shouldn't have told you. My love for you made me mad with terror.

CLITHEROE: *(angrily)* They'll say now that I sent you out th' way I'd have an excuse to bring you home … Are you goin' to turn all th' risks I'm takin' into a laugh?

LIEUT. LANGON: Let me lie down, let me lie down, Bill; th' pain would be easier, maybe, lyin' down … Oh, God, have mercy on me!

CAPT. BRENNAN: *(to Langon)* A few steps more, Jim, a few steps more; thry to stick it for a few steps more.

LIEUT. LANGON: Oh, I can't, I can't, I can't!

CAPT. BRENNAN: *(to Clitheroe)* Are you comin', man, or are you goin' to make an arrangement for another honeymoon? … If you want to act th' renegade, say so, an' we'll be off!

BESSIE: *(from above)* Runnin' from th' Tommies — choke th' chicken. Runnin' from th' Tommies — choke th' chicken!

CLITHEROE: *(savagely to Brennan)* Damn you, man, who wants to act th' renegade? *(to Nora)* Here, let go your hold; let go, I say!

NORA: *(clinging to Clitheroe, and indicating Brennan)* Look, Jack, look at th' anger in his face; look at th' fear glintin' in his eyes … He himself's afraid, afraid, afraid! He wants you to go th' way he'll have th' chance of death sthrikin' you an' missin' him! … Turn round an' look at him, Jack, look at him, look at him! … His very soul is cold … shiverin' with th' thought of what may happen to him … It is his fear that is thryin' to frighten you from recognizin' th' same fear that is in your own heart!

CLITHEROE: *(struggling to release himself from Nora)* Damn you, woman, will you let me go!

CAPT. BRENNAN: *(fiercely, to Clitheroe)* Why are you beggin' her to let you go? Are you afraid of her, or what? Break her hold on you, man, or go up, an' sit on her lap!

Clitheroe tries roughly to break Nora's hold.

NORA: *(imploringly)* Oh, Jack… Jack… Jack!

LIEUT. LANGON: *(agonizingly)* Brennan, a priest; I'm dyin', I think, I'm dyin'!

CLITHEROE: *(to Nora)* If you won't do it quietly, I'll have to make you! *(To Brennan)* Here, hold this gun, you, for a minute. *(He hands the gun to Brennan.)*

NORA: *(pitifully)* Please, Jack … You're hurting me, Jack Honestly … Oh, you're hurting … me! … I won't, I won't, I won't! … Oh, Jack, I gave you everything you asked of me … Don't fling me from you, now!

Clitheroe roughly loosens her grip, and pushes her away from him. Nora sinks to the ground and lies there.

(Weakly) Ah, Jack… Jack… Jack!

CLITHEROE: *(taking the gun back from Brennan)* Come on, come on.

They go out. Bessie looks at Nora lying on the street, for a few moments, then, leaving the window, she comes out, runs over to Nora, lifts her up in her arms, and carries her swiftly into the house. A short pause, then down the street is heard a wild, drunken yell; it comes nearer, and Fluther enters, frenzied, wild-eyed, mad, roaring drunk. In his arms is an earthen half-gallon jar of whiskey; streaming from one of the pockets of his coat is the arm of a new tunic shirt; on his head is a woman's vivid blue hat with gold lacing, all of which he has looted.

FLUTHER: *(singing in a frenzy)*

Fluther's a jolly good fella! … Fluther's a jolly good fella!

Up th' rebels! … That nobody can deny!

(He beats on the door.) Get us a mug or a jug; or somethin', some o' yous, one o' yous, will yous, before I lay one o' yous out! … *(Looking down the street)* Bang an' fire away for all Fluther cares … *(Banging at door)* Come down an' open th' door, some of yous, one o' yous, will yous, before I lay some o' yous out! … Th' whole city can topple home to hell, for Fluther!

Inside the house is heard a scream from Nora, followed by a moan.

FLUTHER: *(singing furiously)*

That nobody can deny, that nobody can deny, For Fluther's a jolly good fella, Fluther's a jolly good fella,

Fluther's a jolly good fella … Up th' rebels! That nobody can deny!

(His frantic movements cause him to spill some of the whiskey out of the jar.) Blast you, Fluther, don't be spillin' th' precious liquor! *(He kicks at the door.)* Ay, give us a mug or a jug or somethin', one o' yous, some o' yous, will yous, before I lay one o' yous out!

The door suddenly opens, and Bessie, coming out, grips him by the collar.

BESSIE: *(indignantly)* You bowsey, come in ower o' that I'll thrim your thricks o' dhrunken dancin' for you, an' none of us knowin' how soon we'll bump into a world we were never in before!

FLUTHER: *(as she is pulling him in)* Ay, th' jar, th' jar, th' jar!

A short pause, then again is heard a scream of pain from Nora. The door opens and Mrs Gogan and Bessie are seen standing at it.

BESSIE: Fluther would go, only he's too dhrunk … Oh, God, isn't it a pity he's so dhrunk! We'll have to thry to get a docthor somewhere.

MRS GOGAN: I'd be afraid to go … Besides, Mollser's terrible bad. I don't think you'll get a docthor to come. It's hardly any use goin'.

BESSIE: *(determinedly)* I'll risk it … Give her a little of Fluther's whiskey … It's th' fright that's brought it on her so soon … Go on back to her, you.

Mrs Gogan goes in, and Bessie softly closes the door. She is moving forward, when the sound of some rifle shots, and the tok, tok, tok of a distant machine-gun bring her to a sudden halt. She hesitates for a moment, then she tightens her shawl round her, as if it were a shield, then she firmly and swiftly goes out.

(As she goes out) Oh, God, be Thou my help in time o' throuble. An' shelter me safely in th' shadow of Thy wings!

Curtain.

Understanding action and structure

The incidents in this extract occur during the Easter Rebellion of 1916, when Irish Nationalists led a rebellion against the British government of the time. Fighting moved away from the Central Post Office to the streets of Dublin and with the street fighting came looting, disorder and tragedy.

In this extract we meet a number of the key characters, some of whom take part in a comic episode of looting, others who are presented in a more tragic manner, such as Lieutenant Langon and Nora.

Looting

- Why does Bessie challenge Mrs Gogan?

- What is Mrs Gogan's response?

- How do we know Fluther has taken part in the looting when he enters at the end of the Act?

Nora and Clitheroe

Look at the section of the play on page 137 from:

'NORA: Jack, Jack, Jack; God be thanked …'

down to

'NORA: I won't, I won't; I promise, I promise, Jack …'

- What does this show us of Nora's feeling at the time?

- Why does Bessie 'risk it' at the end of the extract?

Turmoil in Dublin

- How does O'Casey create a sense of the civil disorder and trouble in Dublin?

- What has happened to Lieutenant Langon?

This play ends with the shooting of Nora when she runs (as a result of her unstable condition brought on by her labour) to the window of her room in the hope of seeing her husband once again.

Understanding character

O'Casey's characters have the mark of real beings who live and breathe. In this short extract we see a number of individuals.

- Make a list of all the characters that appear in the extract.

- Which characters do we feel pity for?

- Which characters are amusing?

- Are there any characters we might admire?

Look at the incident with the woman at the beginning of the extract.

- What is Fluther's excuse for not helping the woman?

- How does Peter deal with the woman?

Understanding themes

The main theme that O'Casey is exploring is the way in which innocent people are affected by the political activity. Despite the fact that the rebellion is one that volunteers such as Clitheroe are happy to get involved in, the consequences are often dreadful.

Look at the following:

> NORA: *(clinging to Clitheroe, and indicating Brennan)* Look, Jack, look at th' anger in his face; look at th' fear glintin' in his eyes … He himself's afraid, afraid, afraid! He wants you to go th' way he'll have th' chance of death sthrikin' you an' missin' him! … Turn round an' look at him, Jack, look at him, look at him! … His very soul is cold … shiverin' with th' thought of what may happen to him … It is his fear that is thryin' to frighten you from recognizin' th' same fear that is in your own heart!
>
> CLITHEROE: *(struggling to release himself from Nora)* Damn you, woman, will you let me go!

- What is Nora saying about Brennan here?
- Why does she say this?

Another theme is the strength of the human spirit and it is Bessie Burgess at the end of the extract that provides this quality when she goes out onto the street to fetch help for Nora.

Understanding dramatic devices

Language

The most obvious feature in the extract is the use of the Dublin dialect of the day. O'Casey's ability to write convincing dialogue in this way has made him one of the most important writers of the twentieth century. He has been very influential and other playwrights, such as Arthur Miller, have expressed their admiration.

Look at the text on page 136 from:

'PETER: *(shouting)* Don't be assin' me to open any door, don't be assin' …'

down to

'PETER: Lowsey bastard, lowsey bastard!'

Write the passage out in standard English and notice the differences in your version and O'Casey's. One important aspect is that it is not just words, but phrases and whole sentences that are different from standard English.

Humour

There is plenty of verbal humour here as well as the more knockabout sort of humour characterised by Fluther and the Covey.

- Find three examples of humour from the extract and use evidence to support your selection.

Juxtaposition

This is a technique where different types of action are present in the same scene. Here, the broad comedy is juxtaposed on the tragic events surrounding Lieutenant Langon, Clitheroe and Nora.

Understanding performance

Acting

There are some wonderful opportunities for acting in this extract. O'Casey provides a huge range of action and emotion which make the play very interesting to watch.

- Why would the characters of Nora, Bessie, Lieutenant Langon and Fluther be a challenge for an actor?

Sound

O'Casey wants us to experience the impact of the street battles in the rebellion of 1916 and part of his technique is to use sound and noise very effectively.

- Find two examples where sound adds to the sense of confusion and danger.

Setting, costume and props

O'Casey's stage directions are very detailed and the setting, costume and props provide an audience with a feast of visual entertainment.

- What is the importance of the pram, the sack of flour, the hat the Fluther wears and Clitheroe's rifle?

Tasks

Personal response: writing

1   Write a short scene where both Fluther and the Covey meet a policeman as they are looting a building.

2   'O'Casey allows us to cry and to laugh at what he presents on stage.' How true do you think this is? You should write about:

a) action

b) characters

c) language

d) any other relevant issues.

Practical activities

Individually or in pairs

3   Write a short comic sketch that uses your local dialect. You may base your sketch on some of the events in *The Plough and the Stars*.

4   Examine Clitheroe's dilemma as a man torn between two forces: loyalty to his wife, and loyalty to his country. Write down three reasons why he should stay with Nora and three why he should go with Brennan.

5   Design a poster for the play.

In groups

6   Allocate parts and act out the extract.

Useful notes

Wrathmines	O'Casey mocks the middle-class Dublin accent
howl	whole
derogatory	a misuse of the word (or malapropism), what Fluther means is 'unfortunate'
sthrict	O'Casey is imitating the working-class Dublin pronunciation
bassinettes	hooded cane or wicker cradles or prams
harp an' shamrock	symbols of Irish nationalism
lion an' unicorn	symbols of the British crown
sky thinkin'	praying and thinking about religion
kinch	stamp or quality
sorra mind I'd mind	it wouldn't bother me
mot's	a moth's
lath	a thin strip of wood used in plastering
slum lice	abusive metaphor for slum dwellers
Minsthrel Boys	Irish patriots (referring to a famous song: 'The Minstrel Boy')
Harps	guns, a reference to Minsthrel Boys (above)
choke th' chicken	a mocking reference to the failure of the Nationalists in the rebellion
Bowsey	drunkard
brought it on her so soon	labour; Nora is pregnant